CLAIM YOUR GIFT!

Thank you for purchasing this novel. For a special behind-the-scenes e-book, including historical background on which *The Sisterhood* was based please visit:

Books.click/Sisterhood

* * *

This e-book companion includes group discussion ideas, unique photographs and much more!

JOIN OUR ONLINE BOOK CLUB!

Book club members receive free books and the hottest pre-release novels. To join our exclusive online book club and discuss *The Sisterhood* with likeminded readers, please visit:

Books.click/DuboisBookclub

* * *

We look forward to see you in our bookclub family!

THE SISTERHOOD: A NOVEL OF TRUE SISTERHOOD

A Novella

By Caroline Dubois

TABLE OF CONTENTS

"Dubois has created the kind of friendship that is not superficial, silly, or a plot sideline, but private, deep, and more real than anything else. It will make your heart sing." **—Daily Telegraph**

* * *

"Wonderful… A wry, sharply observed tale of both heroism and coming-of-age during one of the darkest times of humanity." **— Chicago Sun-Times**

* * *

"Compulsively readable… Dubois has a distinctively contemporary literary voice. The dialogue resounds, and the author's humor gives texture to the prose." **—O, The Oprah Magazine**

* * *

"Biting, brilliant exploration of a female friendship from the eyes of a sensitive author. And though *The Sisterhood* focuses on young women, readers need be neither young nor female in order to enjoy it…" **—Publishers Weekly**

* * *

"Riveting… This short novel is more than an exploration of friendship, it is about what happens when the things we take for granted slip away and we are forced to test our inner strength." **—Daily Mirror**

* * *

"*The Sisterhood* is a 200 page novella yet it manages to cover a heart-wrenching saga… Dubois's hyperaware voice lends the story poignancy and relatability." **—USA Today**

* * *

"Set in WWII war-torn Europe, young Helena and Maria struggle to do what is right in a world where cruelty is the norm. Never boring… this short book is a pageturner." **— SheKnows.com**

* * *

"Wonderful… The novella's depiction of the dynamics of

friendship—how there's often affection and admiration mixed with disappointment and frustration—is uniquely authentic." **—Washington Post**

* * *

"Dubois's portrayal of a true friendship reads like the voice of the charmingly blunt friend you wish you had; the author's observations are sensitive and insightful." **—New York Post**

* * *

"Comedy and pathos are braided together with extraordinary skill in a haunting short novel... riveting intensity and originality" **—Miami Herald**

* * *

"Clever and suspenseful… Dubois captures well the old-school girlfriends' zeitgeist… and this riveting tale will make older readers fondly recall the days when kids got in trouble for passing (print) notes in class." **—People**

* * *

"Dubois captures the complexities, naiveté and angst of teenage girls so well my stomach was in knots. What had happened to Helena Goldstein, the Jewish girl in Nazi Germany? You'll find yourself staying up all night to find out." **—The Atlanta Journal-Constitution**

* * *

"Riveting… I couldn't believe it was based on a true story. I cried and laughed… Dubois does a fine job of building suspense and creating characters, notably Maria and Helena, whom the readers will care about and empathize with." **— PopSugar**

* * *

"Fast-paced and suspenseful… a page-turning story of friendship mixed with a bit of a thriller. Shines a light on the power of true friendship in times of external challenges." **— The New Yorker**

* * *

"A tale of elaborate mystery intertwined with the tenderness of a mother's love, *The Sisterhood* exudes warmth at every turn… Gripping and uplifting, it is a true pageturner." —**The Augusta Chronicle**

* * *

"*The Sisterhood* is interested—almost single-mindedly so—in the friendship between Maria and her friend Helena, two young women who are in the process of discovering that life as an adult in WWII Europe is vastly different than it was as teenagers in the early 1930s. This novella is refreshing in part because it's hugely uninterested in the surrounding characters and focuses on the main two characters, which you are bound to fall in love with…"—**BookPage**

* * *

"Dubois is a gifted documentarian… The story is filled with keenly observed details and depicts the role that outside events plays in the characters' lives." —**Kirkus Reviews**

* * *

"There is a sentimental delight in reading *The Sisterhood* and its roller coaster ride of friendship facing existential threats. In the end, Dubois draws a vivid and convincing portrait of a true friendship." —**Time Magazine**

* * *

"A sharp, funny and uplifting exploration of a 70 years old story about true friendship." —**Bustle**

* * *

"…Admirably, readably realistic—the author knows these girls and the world they live in in the most profound way… Dubois nails the complex blend of love, loyalty, and courage that binds female friends." —**Real Simple Magazine**

* * *

"*The Sisterhood* is a moving, focused, very funny novel, told with a calming amount of perspective by a trustworthy, precise voice. It is intimate and insightful regarding two decades of life (early teens to twenties), and on the topics of endurance (both emotional and physical) in Nazi Occupied Poland." **—RT Book Reviews**

* * *

"Truth-teller Caroline Dubois hurls both heart and mind into this touching, bittersweet tale of the strongest friendship you'll ever read about, based on a true and riveting story." — **Redbook**

* * *

"Dubois traces the lives of the novel's main subjects with unswerving candor and compassion… In the author's telling, neither evil nor good is banal; and if the latter doesn't always triumph, it certainly inspires." **—Dallas Morning News**

* * *

"As chronicled… with unblinking accuracy, their agonies are appalling to contemplate, their stories of survival and friendship under duress enthralling to hear." **—Denver Rocky Mountain News**

* * *

"Haunting account of bravery, friendship, and endurance." — **Huffington Post**

* * *

"Compelling… Dubois weaves into this suspenseful, detailed narrative myriad moments of friendship, challenges, and valor." **—Connecticut Post**

* * *

"Heightened by electrifying and staggering detail, Dubois's riveting story stands as a luminous testament to the indomitable will to survive and the unbreakable bonds of friendship."**—San Francisco Chronicle**

* * *

"Even history's darkest moments can be illuminated by spectacular courage, such as courage that Righteous Among the Nations Medal Recipient, Maria Bozek-Nowak, displayed toward her childhood friend Helena Goldstein… The author has created a detailed account, sensitively rendered, of human triumph."—**Entertainment Weekly**

* * *

"The first complete account of these extraordinary women and, incredibly, over 70 years later we are still learning new and riveting truths about the courage of people during WWII… An important new perspective… Careful research and sensitive retelling." —**Library Journal**

* * *

"As Dubois delves deeply into the two women's fight for survival, the narrative seamlessly comes together in order to share a significant part of history whose time has come to be heard." —**Patriot-Ledger**

* * *

"A miraculous story about friendship and the will to overcome extraordinary heartache and loss. A small wonder of a book." —**Bookish**

* * *

"A book so simple, so seemingly effortless, that it's almost perfect."—**The Guardian**

* * *

"The whole work is seamless, compelling, and memorable—impossible to put down; difficult to forget." —**The Atlantic**

* * *

"Humorous, heartwarming, often nostalgic, *The Sisterhood* captures the spirit of true friendship, one that will bring both laughter and tears to your eyes. Guaranteed." —**BookBub**

* * *

"Fabulous… It is seldom that I read a book that continuously draws me through it with interest. Though I avoid books about The Sisterhood out of discomfort for the empathy I have for Holocaust victims, I was impressed with this uplifting and inspiring story." —**Omnivoracious**

Dedicated to the memory of the
Goldstein and Bozek families

Based on a true story

PART ONE

PROLOGUE

Maria stood in the train station.

It was finally spring.

The war was now over. How long she had been waiting for this moment?

Her hands fidgeted on her purse. She bit her lip. She missed her friend so intensely.

And now she was finally coming. Maria sighed, "The poor girl…"

Who could have imagined things would turn out this way?

Taking a deep breath, she bit her lip again. She shook her head disapprovingly at herself. "You should stop this," she thought, "don't bite your lip that way. It's not ladylike!"

She folded her hands together. "Oh God, bring her here already!"

At the same time on the train approaching the border into the country, a young woman wearing a green dress sat quietly by the window, her thoughts wandering.

It was over.

The war was over.

And now, she could finally return to her beloved city. To her beloved city square, to the famous fountain in front of the city hall. To the many doves there. To the sound of the trams driving slowly on the old streets. To the theatre. To the ballet.

But more than anything, she missed her friend.

The train stopped at the border.

She sat up as border police officers passed in the aisle. She smiled at the officer and handed him her identification papers. Before the war, she knew nothing about these things. One ID was fine. But nowadays, one had to carry multiple forms of identification.

The officer looked at the photo and then at her, "Maria?"

She nodded.

"Date of birth?"

"January 22nd," she said calmly, "1920."

"And what was the purpose of your stay abroad?"

"The war," she murmured.

The officer said nothing and proceeded to look at her birth certificate, her baptism certificate, and her high school graduation diploma. He then nodded and handed them back to her.

She nodded back and put the documents in her file, and tucked it into the front of her suitcase. These very documents saved her so many times in the past three years.

But soon she won't need them any more.

Soon she could return to herself. Her *real* self.

She gazed at the views of the countryside through the window. In a few hours, she'd be there. Her beloved city.

She would see her best friend again. Her savior.

She smiled to herself, gazing at the fields outside. To think, she did not want to be seated next to Maria in class in the first place! How different things could have turned out.

CHAPTER 1

"Helena!"

The harsh tone of Mrs. Schlesinger startled Helena from her daydreams. "Yes, Mrs. Schlesinger!"

"You are going to sit near Maria," Mrs. Schlesinger said and pointed at the desk in the front of the class.

Helena dreaded this day. For the past two weeks, since the school year began, she sat next to Gisele, who was funny, witty and beautiful. The two of them sat at the back of the classroom near the window where Helena could stare out at the sky. She loved looking outside, especially during boring science lessons, and math lessons, and all that nonsense.

She sighed, took her textbooks, and walked to the front of the class, sitting down next to the shy girl, Maria.

Maria stared down at the desk, smiling sheepishly at Helena without looking at her. Trying to smile back, Helena's face formed a grimace, her eyebrows frowning. She sighed. This would be like sitting in a graveyard, she thought.

Mrs. Schlesinger continued to assign new seating arrangements for the students as she had promised on the first day of the school year. Helena looked around the class. She was devastated. She tried her best to make a good impression, hoping the severe-looking Mrs. Schlesinger wouldn't separate her and Gisele. She had known Gisele since elementary school. Gisele was fun, and funny too.

But now Gisele looked forlorn as a new girl, Sofia, was placed in Helena's old seat.

Helena sighed a little too loud. Mrs. Schlesinger gave her a fierce look. Helena lowered her eyes at once.

When Mrs. Schlesinger finished arranging the classroom, the class was quiet. Helena shook her head. Mrs. Schlesinger didn't have a clue what she was doing.

During the break Helena tried to change things. She went to Mrs. Schlesinger in the teacher's room. Mrs. Schlesinger gave her one quick look and said, "Not a chance, Helena!"

"But Mrs. Schlesinger!" Helena pleaded.

"These are the new seating assignments! You would be wise to learn some manners and discipline from Maria!"

Helena tried, "But… *please*, Mrs. Schlesinger!"

But her teacher turned her back to her. The conversation was over.

Feeling desperate, Helena went to Gisele, who was waiting in their favorite spot - the bench in the school yard they had claimed as their own over the past two weeks.

Gisele was also depressed. Her desk was now four rows apart from Helena.

"Perhaps," Helena said, "we could get your parents and my parents to speak to Mrs. Schlesinger?"

Gisele shook her head, "It won't work."

They were silent.

Then Helena said, "What do you know of that girl she put me with?"

"Who? *Maria?*" Gisele asked, "I guess she's... well... I don't really know, I never noticed her before..."

"Exactly," Helena sighed.

Weeks passed and Helena noticed how difficult it was to look out of the window from her new position. Mrs. Schlesinger would tap on her shoulder, or worse, call out her name to get her attention. She was all too visible. All too in the front of the class, along with all the bookworms. She hated it.

To make matters worse, the mute classmate sharing her desk, the Maria girl, was *always* listening and taking notes. She continually nodded but never said a word. She never raised her hand, though

Helena noticed she always wrote the correct answers in her exercise book as if testing herself before the answer was revealed

It drove Helena crazy. One day, after the bell rang, before heading into the yard with Gisele and the others, she asked Maria, "Why don't you raise your hand?"

"Excuse me?" Maria mumbled, looking down.

"Mr. Kissinger asked the square root question and you knew the answer!"

"No I… didn't…"

"Liar," Helena said, "I saw you writing it in your notebook!"

Maria's face reddened. No one ever called her a liar!

But Helena raised her eyebrows knowingly and left the classroom.

Maria stayed frozen to her chair. She was stunned. She gulped and opened the biology book. She wanted to go over her homework and make sure she had done everything correctly.

CHAPTER 2

It was an unlikely friendship. They didn't have anything in common. Helena was perhaps the most popular. Maria was perhaps the least.

During one particular literature lesson, Mrs. Schlesinger asked who would like to read the poem. Helena—happy about the class *finally* becoming interesting—volunteered.

Mrs. Schlesinger asked her to stand in front of the class, and Helena jumped off her seat, grabbed the book and began reading excitedly:

"Stars circle round thy head," she raised her hand above, and then lowered it, "and at thy feet surges the sea, upon whose hurrying waves," she raised her hand again drawing a large arch, "a rainbow glides before thee, cleaving the clouds!"

Maria sat up, mesmerized. All the students were.

"Whate'er thou look'st upon is thine!" Helena continued, "Coasts, ships, men, mountains, cities, all belong to thee!" She shouted, "Master of Heaven as earth, it seems as naught," her voice suddenly turned into a whisper, "could equal thee in glory...!"

She grinned, bowed, and went back to her seat. Everyone cheered.

"Well done," smiled Mrs. Schlesinger.

Later when the bell rang, Maria said to Helena, "That was beautiful."

Helena was somewhat startled by her mute classmate speaking to her. "Uh? Oh, thank you..."

"Have you..." Maria continued, as Helena's eyes grew bigger, noticing this was now the *second* sentence initiated by the mute, "Have you..." Maria searched for words, "You demonstrated so beautifully, Helena, the *sea* and the *waves*... Have you ever *been* to the sea?"

Helena bellowed, "Why, of course! Every summer!" She looked at Maria, "Don't tell me you *haven't*...?"

Maria looked down. Helena was puzzled. What else was there to do in the summer *but* go to a summer house by the sea?

Gisele tapped her on the shoulder. "Are we going or what?"

When they were in the yard, Helena whispered, "Could you believe it, Gisele? I think Maria has never been to the sea!"

Gisele shrugged her shoulders.

"But," Helena exclaimed, "not going to the sea? What else can she do each summer?"

Gisele smiled, "Not everyone goes to a summer house, Helena!"

"But *you* do!" Helena exclaimed.

"Yes, but not *everyone*." She lowered her voice. "Maria's father works for the railroad, and I heard that her mother works in some factory, you see? They don't have much money…"

Helena's eyes grew bigger, "But she's so… *dignified*… and *smart*…!"

"Well," Gisele shook her head, "that's because she's a bookworm. But," she whispered, "she's very poor. Didn't you see how her lunch is always only bread and a boiled egg, nothing else?"

Helena was baffled.

Gisele laughed, "Close your mouth. You'll swallow a fly."

The following lesson was biology. Helena didn't care about chromosomes and genes. She wrote in her notebook, "Have you NEVER been to the sea? Seriously??"

She slid her notebook over to Maria.

Maria glanced at the notebook and quickly looked back at Mr. Kissinger. She gently pushed Helena's notebook away.

Helena was stunned. Did that girl just push her notebook away? Did she just refuse to *talk* to her? That couldn't be! She took her pen and drew a big question mark in the center of her notebook, then slid it again toward Maria.

Maria gulped. She bit her lip. She didn't want to miss a word from Mr. Kissinger's lecture. But, she had to admit, she already knew everything he was saying. He was just repeating what was in the textbook. She had read it. She knew it.

"No," she wrote on her own notebook. She slowly moved it for Helena to see. Her heart beat faster. She felt like she was committing a crime.

"SERIOUSLY?" Helena wrote in capital letters. "What do you do in the SUMMER???"

Maria bit her lip. She kept looking at Mr. Kissinger, her heart pounding, and wrote, in her small handwriting "babysitting." She *wanted* to write, "I take care of my young brother and sister," but it would have taken too much time.

Helena was puzzled and whispered, "Really…?"

"Helena and Maria!" Mr. Kissinger exclaimed, "To the principal's office! Right now!"

A murmur passed through the class. Maria's eyes widened. Had he just called her name?

Mr. Kissinger wrote them a small note and handed it to Helena with gusto, "Go!"

Helena stood up, her chin held high, and walked out of the class.

Maria, wide-eyed, looked at Mr. Kissinger in utter horror.

He raised his eyebrows, "You heard me!"

Maria's legs felt heavy, her knees buckling. She got up and slowly walked out of class. This had *never* happened to her. Never!

The school's secretary told the two girls to sit and wait in the hallway.

Maria thought of her mother. What would she think? How would she respond?

She began to weep.

Helena put her arm around Maria's shoulder, "Hey! Don't cry, it will be fine…!"

Maria's shoulder quivered as she buried her face in her hands.

"Wait…" Helena said slowly, "is this your first time?"

Maria nodded her head vigorously.

"Oh…" Helena said, "don't worry about it, they just write something in a book, and its all fine. We'll be back in class in a moment."

Maria shook her head, "I shouldn't… I shouldn't have…."

Helena thought of something to say to distract the poor girl from crying. "Do you," she finally said, "really *babysit?*"

Maria nodded and wiped her tears, "My two younger siblings…"

"No!" Helena's eyes shone. "You have *two*

younger siblings? I always wanted to have younger siblings! Girls? Boys?"

Maria sniffled, "A boy, Eddie, and a girl, Sashinka—I mean—Sasha…"

"Wow!" Helena jumped off her seat, "A boy *and* a girl! Wow! Which one do you like best?"

Maria tilted her head, "I don't know…"

"Sure you do!"

Maria smiled through her teary eyes, "I guess… Eddie can be really annoying at times. But I can speak to him… Sasha is too young, but she's as sweet as a candy!"

Helena sat down and sighed, "I wish I had little siblings."

Maria looked at her, "You don't have any…?"

"Oh, I do have two brothers, but they're older. My eldest brother, Solomon, he has a girlfriend now. Her name's Hannah!"

Maria nodded.

"And my other brother, Reuben, he'd do anything for me. They both spoil me to bits."

"Really?" Maria whispered, "You must feel so lucky."

"Lucky? Hell no! I wish I had little ones. I would *play* with them, and *dance* with them, and *sing* with them…"

The principal's secretary called their names. She looked at them disapprovingly, "The principal is busy…"

Taking a big breath, Helena said excitedly: "Mrs. Burtman, I just asked Maria about the chromosome because there was something I didn't understand, you see, and I didn't want to stop Mr. Kissinger's flow, because when he begins talking, he never stops, you see, and so I asked Maria and she just tried to explain it to me, and when he called our names, I *tried* to explain to him that Maria was just explaining to me about the chromosome, but he would have none of it, and it's too bad, you see, because had he *asked*, he'd see that not everyone understands what he says, in *fact*…"

"Alright, alright," Mrs. Burtman sighed, and signed the slip of paper. She looked at Helena, and then at Maria, "Don't do this again! Now hurry back to class!"

Helena grinned, "Thank you so much, Mrs. Burtman. You won't regret it!"

Helena grabbed Maria's hand, and they ran down the hall. Then, out of sight of the principal's office, Helena began climbing the stairs to the third floor.

"But," Maria asked, bewildered, "aren't we going back to—"

Helena smiled, "No! There are only a few more minutes before the class ends. We'll go to my favorite spot…"

"But," Maria gasped, looking nervously around, "I… What will Mr. Kissinger…—"

"Mr. Kissinger wouldn't like us coming back now and interrupting his speech, right?"

Maria stammered, "Bu… But…"

"And you know," Helena continued, "how the other kids would whisper and get all excited when we come back, and Mr. Kissinger, well, this will upset him!"

"I… I…"

"Come on already!"

Once they reached the top floor, Helena opened a large window, stretched her leg over the ledge, and climbed onto the roof. She reached for Maria's hand.

Maria pulled her hand back, "I'm not… I can't...!"

"Of course you can. Give me your hand!"

Maria gulped and looked at the empty hallway around her.

Helena pressed, "Give me your hand!"

Maria gave her hand to Helena, placed her leg on the ledge, and then stretched her other leg out. The view was frightening. She could see the whole schoolyard below, as well as the street and the top of the trees. She gasped. The roof tile under her foot groaned. She looked at Helena, "Are you sure it's...—"

"Positive," Helena smiled. She squatted on the roof tiles and moved away from the window. "Here," she whispered, "if we squeeze here, no one can see us from the corridor!"

Maria squeezed into the small place. "How did you find this place?"

"In my old school," Helena said, "I knew *all* the spots. My favorite one was in the theatre's dressing room... Oh, it was truly magical!"

Maria smiled. The view was both frightening and exciting. A wrong move could cause them to tumble down. But the view was breathtaking. She had never been so high in her life.

"...And when this school year started," Helena continued, "the first thing I did was to look for quiet spots..."

Maria was surprised, "But I thought you always like to be around the other pupils."

Helena shrugged her shoulders, "I'd much rather be around good books. Or poems. Or plays!"

Maria's eyes widened. "I thought you only... that you only like to be with everyone around you..."

Helena shrugged her shoulders again, "Yes and no."

Maria nodded. She liked that answer. Yes and no.

They sat quietly.

Maria wanted to ask about Helena's brothers. And which books she liked reading. And what her favorite subject was. She liked it when Helena talked. But now she was quiet. They looked at the buildings in the horizon from the view of the roof. Each of them hugged her knees to her chest. Then Helena sighed. Maria did the same. She wanted to be as carefree as Helena.

A few minutes later, Helena said, "I think we should go back."

Maria nodded. They crawled slowly to the window, climbed inside and closed the window behind them. They hurried downstairs and entered their class just as the bell rang. The children turned to look at them, excited. Mr. Kissinger frowned. Grabbing his bag, he took the note from Helena's hand, giving them both a glare, and stormed out of the classroom.

"Helena, how was it?" one of the children asked. "What did the principal say?" asked another. "Did he suspend you?" asked the third.

Soon a small circle formed around Helena and Maria. Helena related the events as Maria looked at the floor, embarrassed yet exhilarated by the attention.

But then she noticed the homework assignment written on the blackboard and returned to the desk to write the homework down.

Helena looked at her and exclaimed, "Oh, stop it! Let's go out!"

Maria's eyes widened. "But, the homework…!"

Helena shook her head. She glanced over to Gisele and Isabella who were waiting near the door. She whispered into Maria's ear, "It's not as if you didn't read the whole book already!"

Maria shrugged her shoulders. Helena grabbed her hand. "Come!"

CHAPTER 3

Soon after their incident with Mr. Kissinger, there was a day when Helena was ill and did not come to school. Maria felt like the class was dead without Helena's presence. She sent a note with Gisele, wishing Helena a quick recovery.

Two days later, when Helena returned, she hugged Maria. "Thank you for your note!"

Maria enjoyed being hugged like this. She was not accustomed to embraces. She was discovering Helena was always like that: hugging, giggling, dramatic. She always saw opportunities, solutions, and ways of turning a dull moment truly magical.

In class they sometimes wrote to one another in their notebooks. Maria never liked it, but sometimes it did help making a boring lesson a little livelier.

During breaks she always joined Helena and the girls. Doing her best to imitate the other girls by nodding and laughing, she hid the fact she didn't enjoy all the conversations. The ones about the boys embarrassed her. But she tried.

One morning, when they were returning to class after break, Helena pulled Maria closer, "I have a ballet performance!"

"A ballet performance?"

"Yeah, nothing too big. But I would love for you to come and watch!"

"I… when is it?"

"Tomorrow at five!"

"But… I… I can't…" Maria sighed, "I have to be with my siblings. My parents only return home at seven… Oh, I wish I could, Helena!"

"But Maria!" Helena exclaimed, "This is a big performance for me. You *must* come!"

"But… What will I do with Eddie and Sasha?"

"Bring them with you! The performance is free to attend!"

"I'm… I'm… not sure if my mother will let me."

"Sure she would!" They entered class and sat down. "Just don't pose it as a question, Maria. Announce it to her!"

Maria shook her head, "I can't. I'm not like *you!*"

"Of course you are! Tell your mother that you can either go for the performance *and* stay for the dinner afterwards, or that you could just come for the performance and miss the dinner."

"I…" Maria shifted uncomfortably, "she wouldn't let me, Helena!"

"Maria, Maria, Maria…" Helena smiled. "Trust me. Tell her the same way I've told you. Give her these two options, and she'll pick the one that is least worst for her. If you ask her if you can go or not, of course she'll say no!" Helena dropped her voice to a whisper as Mrs. Schlesinger walked into the class, "But if you ask her if you could stay for the dinner or not, she'll have to allow you to go to the performance at the very least!"

The following day, Maria exclaimed to Helena, "You're a magician!"

"She said yes?!"

"She did!"

"Marvelous! A few others from the class will come too. I'm so excited that you'll be there!"

Holding her young brother's one hand, and her toddler sister by the other hand, Maria climbed on the tram. Though it was only four o'clock, it was already getting dark. All of them, bundled into their coats, sat down. She lifted Sasha onto her lap so that she could see outside. It was exciting.

They disembarked near the theatre. On entering the theatre's foyer, Maria spotted Gisele, Isabella, Sofia, and a few others from school.

"Goodness, Maria!" Gisele exclaimed, "you brought your siblings with you!"

"I…" Maria said, trying to look for the right words, "I had to be with—"

Isabella exclaimed, "It's such a brilliant idea! I should have brought my little sister. She would have loved it!"

Gisele nodded, "So considerate of you to bring them…"

Soon Maria became the center of attention as the other girls exclaimed, "They are *so* cute!"

A woman approached Maria, "You must be Maria, darling. I'm Helena's mother."

"Oh, pleased to meet you, Mrs. Goldstein!"

"Oh, darling, you are so kind. I'm so glad you could come! Helena said she was excited about you coming!"

"Did she…?"

At that moment, Maria was interrupted by a spoon tapping on glass as one of the mothers asked everyone to enter the auditorium.

The performance was dazzling. Maria loved every moment of it, as did Eddie and Sasha. Biting her lip nervously, Maria tensed as Helena did some turns—she was afraid Helena would fall—but Helena finished them triumphantly, raising her arms up high and giving her stunning smile.

After the performance, everyone waited for the dancers to come out while they talked with their ballet teacher. Maria looked at the big clock. It was six thirty. She promised her mother she'd be home before seven. She decided to wait for only five more minutes as she rocked tired Sasha in her arms.

After five minutes passed, Maria helped Eddie and Sasha with their coats and hats. She quietly left without saying a word and headed towards the tram station.

Sasha cried, "But you said we'll meet Helena!"

"Oh Sashinka, we'll see her next time."

"But I wanted to see her now," Sasha cried.

They suddenly heard a voice behind them, "Maria!"

Helena ran out of the theatre still wearing her tutu.

"Helena!" Maria exclaimed. She stuttered, "You're... You're not dressed, you'll get sick!"

"I just wanted," Helena said, panting, "to say hello to you all. You must be Eddie, right?"

Eddie nodded.

"And you," Helena said to Sasha, "must be the one and only: Princess Alexandra!"

Sasha smiled, shyly burying her face in Maria's neck.

Maria saw Helena shivering, "Go now, Helena!"

"Okay," Helena said, "but I wanted to thank you so much for coming. It means the world to me!"

Maria smiled. "Go!"

Later, on the tram back home, Maria suddenly realized she had not said anything to Helena about her performance. She sighed and said to herself, 'Ignorant fool!' She should have at least said *something*, about how stunning Helena was, how poised, how majestic, how beautiful!

At home, after she endured her mother's scolding for being late and after dinner was over and her siblings were in bed, Maria sat in the kitchen and wrote Helena a note. She decorated it with flowers and wrote:

> *"To Helena, thank you for a brilliant performance. It was truly magical! Maria"*

She smiled to herself. Helena always used the words, "Truly magical."

Sometime before the end of the school year Maria was sick. She did not come to school, which was unlike her.

Helena asked everyone but no one knew why Maria was not at school. Helena then decided that if Maria would not come to school the following day as well, she'd visit her.

The following day Maria did not come. Helena, who was always rather worry-free, began to fret. She asked the other girls where Maria lived. No one knew exactly, only that she lived near the rail station heading east.

Helena went to the school's secretary. "Mrs. Burtman, I have to find out Maria Bozek's address!"

Armed with the address in hand, Helena skipped school. She shook her head as she left, knowing she'd miss Mr. Kissinger and his boring amoeba and cell formation lectures. But she knew that without Maria's interest in the lesson, she'd be even more lost than usual.

She took the tram to the eastern part of town. She found the street. It was dreary, filled with plain-looking houses. She walked down the street lined with small houses, looking at the numbers. Then she stopped and looked at her slip of paper – this was it.

She knocked on the door.

There was no answer.

She knocked again.

No answer.

She felt aggravated. She knocked forcefully on the door, shouting, "Maria? Maria, it's me, Helena!"

Maria's puzzled voice came from the other side of the door, "*Helena…?*"

"Yes! Open up!"

The door opened instantly. Maria gasped, "What on earth are you—"

Helena embraced her, "I thought something

happened to you! You never missed a day, and now you missed two!"

Maria smiled. She looked pale.

"My god," Helena exclaimed, "you don't look well." She followed Maria down the hallway and into the living room. The house was dark. "Let's open the curtains… How are you feeling?"

"I'm… I'm fine…"

"Well you certainly don't look fine!"

Maria lay on one of the three long sofas, her hand holding her belly.

Helena clapped her hands, "No, let's go to your room. I'll take care of you! Do you want some tea?"

Maria shook her head, "No, thank you."

"I will take it as a yes!" Helena said, walking into the tiny kitchen. She filled a kettle with water and turned on the gas. She called to Maria, "In a moment you'll have some tea…"

Maria murmured a quiet, "Thank you…"

Helena came to the living room and sat down on the opposite sofa, "But why are you lying here, let's go to your room…"

Maria tried smiling, "This… is where we sleep. That's Eddie's bed," she pointed at where Helena was sitting, "and this is my bed. And that's Sashinka's."

"Oh," Helena said, and felt terribly stupid, "I… *knew* that…"

She felt awkward, "I guess I meant…" she shook

her head, "How are you feeling?"

"I'm fine, I'm… fine…"

Helena moved and sat on Maria's bed. "Here, let me see. Do you have a fever?"

Maria shook her head.

"No," Helena concluded, "you don't have a fever. Does your throat hurt? Here, open your mouth…"

Maria laughed, "I'm not going to open… *I'm fine!*"

Helena smiled. "Is it your belly?"

Maria shrugged her shoulders, "I guess."

"I knew it! You ate something bad…"

"No, it's not that…"

"Then what is it?"

Maria shrugged her shoulders again.

Helena sighed. The sound of the boiling kettle broke the silence. "Well, we'll make you some tea and you'll feel just like new!"

She removed the whistling kettle from the stove and made two cups of tea. She looked around the small kitchen, crammed with the sink, an oven and a stove, and a small table with five chairs around it. She shouted, "It is certainly cozy here! What a lovely kitchen!"

Maria grimaced.

Helena brought two cups of tea, placing them on the small living room table. She noticed a blanket on the floor, covering a towel. The room looked messy.

She got up and began folding some of the clothes thrown around and opened the curtains.

Maria sighed.

When Helena came to the blanket thrown on the floor, Maria grabbed to it, "No, please don't…"

Helena saw the towel underneath it, "Oh my God!" she exclaimed, "Dearest Maria!"

Maria covered her face with her hands.

"Dearest Maria!" Helena exclaimed, "You're a woman now! Congratulations!" she jumped around the room, "I can't believe it, I'm so happy for you!"

Maria's face reddened, "Shhh…" she whispered, "you want to shout it to the whole street?!"

"Why not! What a blessing! You are now a w-o-m-a-n!" Helena collapsed dramatically onto the bed, "My mother would be so *happy* for you! What a celebration!"

Maria stared at her. Was Helena *out of her mind?* What was there to *celebrate?*

"Tell me tell me," Helena begged, "how does it *feel*…?"

Maria sighed, "It… hurts… my belly…"

"Of course!" Helena exclaimed, "That's because one day you could have a *baby*, and now your cycle is… um… disappointed for not having a baby, so it goes away!" Helena sat up and sipped her tea, as joyful as ever.

Maria looked at her, puzzled.

Helena looked at her face, "Your mother told you about the whole…"

Maria shook her head.

Helena's eyes grew larger, "Did your mother not…"

Maria shrugged her shoulders.

"What?!" Helena exclaimed, spilling some tea, "Are you telling me your mother didn't tell you what was *going on?* Wait," she hesitated, "Maria, does she… know…?"

Maria shrugged her shoulders, "She just thinks I have some tummy ache…"

"This is…" Helena jumped up, "ex… exasperating!" She walked around the room, "Maria! She needs to *know*, and you must get yourself a… menstrual apron, for these days every month…! I can't believe your *mama* didn't tell you!"

Maria stared at the carpet.

"Well," Helena said, sitting down again, "my mother gave me this talk two years ago! But as for me… it hasn't come yet… Oh… I wish it'd come. She told me we'll go shopping together and celebrate…"

Helena looked at Maria. She was biting her lip. She decided she must explain to her the little she knew. She stood up, mimicking her own mother, "I guess I must tell you what every woman should know."

Maria buried her face in her hands, "No, please don't!"

"Now-now," Helena said, trying to remember her mother's words, "there's nothing to be *ashamed* of. This means that your body has *ripened* and is ready for the *art of reproduction*...! Which only means that for *now*, for many years, until you are an old woman, you'll be... um... *visited* by this... a... splendid visitation! Sometimes it will hurt..." she nodded, reciting her mother's explanation, "but you will get used to it! It is a blessing from God as it means that you have finally come of age!"

Maria blushed and shook her head disapprovingly, her eyes closed.

"Now," Helena said, "we'll have to tell your mother, and make sure she gets you some menstrual aprons, or one of those pads, you know..."

"I'm..." Maria whispered, "I'm not going to wear *that!*"

"Sure you will! What are you going to do, sit around the house once every month for the rest of your *life?*"

Maria shrugged her shoulders and covered her face in her hands again, "I don't know!"

"Well, Gisele already got hers, and so did Isabella!"

Maria peered between her fingers, "Impossible!"

Helena smiled and nodded.

Maria's eyes widened in surprise, "Gisele?! Isabella?!"

Helena nodded, "I've been praying to get mine soon, but the doctor had said it will take more time..."

48

"You... spoke about it with your doctor?"

"Yes, she's a *wonderful* doctor. My mother took me to her. And she said that it will take some time. Look," Helena whispered, "you already have some real breasts budding, and I don't even...—"

Maria now covered her face in her pillow. Helena reached over and pulled it away, "Now-now we must be able to talk about this like ladies!"

Maria reddened, "I can't... believe... we're *talking* about *this!*"

"Well believe it! Sooner or later we'll *have* to! You've seen the funny little hairs under Roman's nose, and Alexander's voice change... We have our share too!"

At that moment the door opened. A rough woman's voice was heard, "Why isn't the door locked! Maria, I told you a thousand times..."

"Mama," Maria exclaimed, "I have a guest!"

A tough-looking woman appeared through the small corridor, she looked at Helena. "Who are you?"

Helena reached her hand cordially, "Helena Goldstein, Madam!" she bowed, "And you must be Mrs. Bozek. I'm most honored to meet you!"

Mrs. Bozek looked at her suspiciously, "You're the dancer."

Helena looked at Maria and grinned, "Aspiring dancer, Madam. *And* actress, and singer too!"

Mrs. Bozek muttered something under her breath. She looked at Maria, "How is your tummy? Could you collect Sasha from kindergarten?"

Maria tried to say something, but her voice broke.

Helena jumped, sensing the complicated situation, "I…"

Maria and her mother both stared at Helena. She took the plunge and said, "Congratulations, Mrs. Bozek!"

She reached and shook the mother's hands firmly, "I believe that your daughter has received it."

"Received what?"

Maria mumbled, "*Oh God…*"

"Well," Helena said, "Mrs. Bozek," she exclaimed, "she had received it. It-it. *It!*"

Mrs. Bozek's eyes suddenly widened. "Oh!"

Helena smiled at her, her big smile, anticipating.

"Oh," Mrs. Bozek said again and frowned, "well… That's quite *early…*"

"No it isn't!" Helena said and sat down, "A few girls in our class have already received it... My mother keeps waiting for me to receive it, Mrs. Bozek…—"

"Does she?" Mrs. Bozek said, looked at her daughter, and sighed. She looked around the room and began folding the few clothes. "Well," she groaned, "what else would she say, that mother of yours?"

"Well," Helena said, looking puzzled at Mrs. Bozek and at Maria, who was hiding her face in her hands, "she'd say… '*Congratulations*' and she'd get me the needed… *equipment*… to… *deal* with… the *situation…"*

Mrs. Bozek groaned, "I see," and quickly disappeared into the kitchen.

Helena leaned toward Maria and whispered, "*Should I go…?"*

Maria's eyes widened, "No! Please don't! I'm so glad you are here!"

They heard Mrs. Bozek's voice from the kitchen, "Well," she shouted and paused, "I better go and collect Sasha before I am too late." She passed by the living room, "Do lock the door, Maria, I beg you!"

"I will, Mama," Maria murmured.

The door closed.

Helena motioned to Maria to keep lying down. She hurried to the door and locked it. She sighed to herself. Wow, what a mother. She didn't say a thing!

When she entered the living room again she put on a big smile, "Well, we *must* celebrate, Maria!"

Maria sighed. "Right now I can't imagine doing anything…"

"Oh please, Maria! It must not be all *that* bad!"

Maria frowned. "It doesn't feel… right."

Helena breathed in. "Well, I guess… that in due time you will start liking it, no?"

"I doubt it."

Helena wanted to say something to cheer her friend up. "Well, you have certainly been missed in school."

Maria snorted, "No one probably noticed I…—"

"Of course! Everyone noticed!"

"You are very kind to me, Helena."

"Well," Helena searched for words, "Mr. Kissinger looked for your approving eyes… And he stared at me with constant disappointment!"

Maria laughed, "I don't give him 'approving eyes'…"

"Of course you do," Helena laughed, "you are the only one actually *listening* to him. He only speaks to you!"

"No he doesn't! Roman listens as well!"

"Well, maybe Roman too, but that's it!"

They smiled.

Silence ensued. This was a little odd. Sure, they were friends. But they weren't *good* friends. Helena tried to think, what would she speak about with Gisele?

She knew the answer. Gisele was mostly into the boys. But Maria always seemed so… shy, about this kind of thing.

Finally, Maria spoke. "What… what did you study, with Mrs. Schlesinger?"

"Right!" Helena jumped up, "We learned 'Captain, O Captain.' Do you want me to recite it to you?"

Maria smiled and nodded.

"O Captain!" Helena exclaimed, "My Captain! Our fearful trip is done, the ship has weather'd every rack, the prize we sought is won... The port is near," she put her hand to her ear, "...the bells I hear, the people all exulting, while follow eyes the steady keel, the vessel grim and daring..."

She grabbed to her chest, "But O heart! Heart! Heart!"

Maria laughed, "Three 'hearts'?!"

Helena nodded excitedly, "But O heart! Heart! Heart! O the bleeding drops of red, where on the deck my Captain lies," she fell down on the sofa, "Fallen... cold... and dead."

Maria clapped, "Terrific!"

Helena smiled, "Then there's something about 'Rise up' and 'hear the bells', but I don't remember it..."

"But you memorized the whole first stanza!"

"Yeah," Helena shrugged her shoulders, "I also memorized the end, 'From fearful trip the victor ship comes in with object won; Exult O shores, and ring O bells! But I," Helena got up again, "with mournful tread... Walk the deck my Captain lies... fallen... cold... and dead...'"

"Bravo!" Maria laughed.

There was a knock at the door.

Helena said, "I'll get it."

Maria jumped, "No, please, no!" and ran to the door. She unlocked it. "Mama! Sashinka!"

Mrs. Bozek handed Maria her young sister. "Now I must go back to work."

Helena, in the living room, heard the conversation at the door. 'Say something,' she prayed, 'you are her *mother* for God's sake, *say* something!'

"I will see you at seven, Maria. Make sure Eddie does his homework."

"Yes Mama."

The door closed.

"Now Sashinka," Maria leaned down and said, "I have a surprise for you in the living room! Guess who is here?!"

CHAPTER 4

A few days later during Mr. Kissinger's class, Helena wrote to Maria in her notebook: "I want to take you out on Sunday."

She gently rotated her notebook for Maria to see.

Maria wrote back in her own notebook, "Can't." She rotated her notebook but then quickly rotated it back and wrote: "Sorry."

Helena drew her usual large question mark, drawing it and thickening its curved line several times.

Maria bit her lip. She kept listening to Mr. Kissinger's words. By now they were both more trained. And Mr. Kissinger, too, seemed more relaxed. Perhaps he had lost hope.

Maria wrote in her small handwriting, "Will be with my family. Sorry…"

Helena wrote, "You need to…" and then drew balloons and fireworks. "My mom said she'll take us both shopping!"

Maria pursed her lips and sighed. It sounded so

good and so much fun.

Helena wrote, "Sunday! Surely you don't have to babysit on *SUNDAYS!*"

"No," Maria wrote, "but my mother won't like it…"

Helena anticipated this. She appreciated Maria's honesty. "Tell her," she wrote, while nodding a little too enthusiastically at Mr. Kissinger's speech about plasma and red blood cells, "that you have to HELP me with the MATH EXAM next Tuesday."

Maria read and gulped.

"Either that," Helena wrote, "or you could come and sleep over at my house on Monday. Either way. This way she will let you go."

Maria shook her head and frowned.

Mr. Kissinger looked at the two of them, and they both quickly lowered their heads.

When the danger passed and Mr. Kissinger was scribbling on the blackboard, Maria wrote, "Let me see."

"I see it as a YES." Helena wrote, and then embellished the "YES".

That Sunday Helena's mother took them both shopping. Maria tried to resist Mrs. Goldstein's offer to buy her a dress. But Mrs. Goldstein said plainly, "Don't insult me, young lady! When someone offers to give you something nice you simply say, 'Thank you very much.' And that's it."

Maria nodded, her heart pounding, "Thank you very much Mrs. Goldstein."

"You are most welcome!" Mrs. Goldstein said cheerfully.

The dress looked stunning and was incomparable to anything Maria had ever worn. It was expensive, too. Helena smiled at her. "It compliments your eyes, Maria!"

Maria was more embarrassed than ever.

They then proceeded to a local pharmacy. Maria loved seeing all the bottles and jars spread across the counter. But when she heard Mrs. Goldstein asking the man for a menstrual apron and twenty pads, she immediately pulled Helena out of the store. Helena exclaimed to her mother, "We'll wait for you outside, Mama!"

"Good, I'll be there in a moment."

Outside, Maria covered her face in her hands, "Oh dear, this is so embarrassing!"

"No it isn't, Maria!"

Mrs. Goldstein exited the pharmacy smiling and handed Maria the bag.

Maria whispered, "Thank you Mrs. Goldstein, very much."

Mrs. Goldstein smiled. Helena jumped, "Soon will be my turn, right mama?"

"Everything in its due time, darling."

CHAPTER 5

As the school year came to an end, Helena extracted a promise from Maria to write to her at the Goldstein family's summer house. She also made Gisele and the others promise that.

But Helena was surprised a few days after they arrived at the summer house, when the family's servant handed her father his letters and then said, "And this, young Miss Goldstein, is for you."

Her eyes grew wide as she received the letter in her hands. She recognized Maria's handwriting. "Oh my!" she exclaimed, "I received a letter! I received a *letter!*" She ran to the balcony, "Solomon! Reuben! I received a letter!"

"Who from?" Reuben shouted at her as she ran back into the house.

"My friend Maria!"

Lying on her bed, she carefully opened the letter. Whilst she had wished for Gisele and Isabella and Sofia to have written, it was Maria who had sent the first letter.

"Dearest Helena,"

Helena read slowly, her chest rising up and down,

> "It's been three days since the beginning of the summer break, and I think of you often. Yesterday I sang to Sashinka and Eddie the song you taught me, of the Queen of the Night… It was great. I couldn't quite sing it like you, but we had lots of fun in the living room, while I dressed up in black, trying to hit those soprano notes of yours…"

Helena grinned and leaned her back against the wall.

> "The city feels empty. Especially without you. I think of you and your brothers having fun at the sea, and, while I refrain from being jealous, I must admit that I wish I could be with you and see the sea as well...
>
> Sashinka prepared some food with me today in the kitchen, and we had lots of fun. Eddie is with his new Karl May book, reading and pretending to be an American cowboy. He's so funny…
>
> Promise me you'll look into the math assignment early on, and not leave it to the end of the summer. I found that for me, bit by bit every day is the best. Don't put it off!
>
> Tell me everything. About the sea, shore, and the sand... In fact everything else too!
>
> I hope I wrote well (surely not as artistically

as you!).

Fondly yours,

Maria Bozek."

Helena stood up, then sat down, then lay down and smiled. She read the letter again, lavishing each word. This letter was for *her*. For her *only!*

She quickly pulled out her notebook from the desk drawer and sat back on the bed. She turned to the middle pages, where she could pull out some paper without damaging the notebook. She wrote:

"Dearest Maria!"

She then embellished the writing with cursive twirls, adding a few stars next to the line,

> "It was such a pleasant surprise to receive your kind letter. I feel glad to hear you like the Queen of the Night. I'm sure Mozart would have been most pleased to hear it!
>
> Mind you, I don't sing it very well either. I do hope to one day after enough training! My singing teacher said that one famous singer, when she finished that whole aria of ten minutes, collapsed on stage! And she also said that Mozart designed it that way! To "pull out your soul!"
>
> I disagree though, dearest Maria. I think he designed it to evoke emotion. If that requires writing the most complicated of arias, then, he was willing to do so. But not to make the singer faint! If anything, he might have wanted the audience to faint!"

Helena looked at the letter. She frowned. It was so boring.

She decided to start anew. She pulled out another piece of paper from the notebook.

"Dearest Maria,"

This time she didn't invest as much time in the twirls. She felt a little guilty about that. But then she concentrated and wrote:

"Your letter finds me well."

Good. She liked the sound of it. She went on.

"It was splendid to read of your adventures with Sashinka and Eddie. You have such a lovely family. The fact that you could sing to them is incredible. Whenever I sing to Reuben or Solomon, they most often roll their eyes.

Solomon thinks of Hannah all the time.

And Reuben, too, I bet you, is thinking of some girl as well. I've seen how eager he was to go to the beach and look at all the women there. I told him he should close his mouth so that he won't drool. But he didn't like my comment!"

Helena smiled and sighed. She continued writing.

"I like it here. I especially like that my father is around more. Back in the city he is busy all the time. Here he reads the newspaper. Sure, don't be mistaken. He did bring with him quite a few folders from the office. But he's also available. Somewhat.

My mother is the happiest. And so am I."

Helena wanted to write more. But she didn't know what to write. This was odd. In the books, whenever she'd read about such correspondence between friends, she thought that had *she* been partaking in such correspondence, she would fill pages and pages.

She thought of writing about a boy she saw on the beach, who reminded her of Alexander.

But it wasn't proper. Not for a letter at least. Besides, Maria wasn't that kind of girl.

She thought of writing about a novel she was reading. But she thought that would be boring.

She thought of writing about how much she missed everyone in class. But the truth was that she didn't *really* miss anyone. Not yet.

And so, she spent two more days trying to figure out what to write. This became her obsession. She even skipped lunch one day trying to think of what to write in her room.

Two days later her mother finally said, "Helena darling, just send the letter as it is. Don't worry about it any more."

"But Mama, it's only one page!"

"Better short and concise than long and melodramatic, darling."

Helena grimaced. This task had become overly difficult. If she needed to write a long fairy tale about two siblings separated in some mysterious circumstances, she would have completed it in a couple of hours! But this whole *letter thing* was not as easy as she had expected.

Finally, she took the piece of paper which had accompanied her to the beach, every meal and even to bed, and wrote on it,

> "P.S.
> I searched for what else to write. I wish I knew what to add! But I see that each day makes the letter older and also further away from you, dearest Maria. So I will let the letter go as it is. This does NOT show my utter appreciation for your kindness to have addressed me here. Please do so again as soon as you receive this letter! I hope that by then I would know what to write to you next time!
>
> Until then, faithfully yours,
>
> Helena Goldstein."

She added her swirly new signature, one on which she worked for hours and hours during Mr. Kissinger's lessons. It was perfect. Almost.

CHAPTER 6

Maria waited to open the letter until evening. She wanted to have time alone, and she wanted to read it when she was concentrating and able to respond right away. She sat in the kitchen and excitedly opened the precious letter.

"Dearest Maria,"

She loved seeing Helena's handwriting. It had been ten days since the end of the school year, and there were still fifty-two days ahead.

She always loved school as she loved learning. But now she also missed school for other reasons, such as seeing her neighbor's beautiful handwriting as she was practicing her twirling signature again and again in her notebook.

She smiled to herself and looked at the signature. She didn't want to hurry. She saw it was only one page, and wanted to linger on each word. She remembered how she had once asked Helena, "How many times do you intend to write that signature of yours?"

Helena was not taken aback. "Why until it's perfect, of course! I'll have to sign it thousands of times, you understand? So I must practice!"

Maria loved that answer. It was so Helena.

As she loved the twirling and the little stars next to her own name. "Dear Maria." The way Helena wrote her name, "Maria", made her feel special.

> "Your letter finds me well. It was splendid to read of your adventures with Sashinka and Eddie. You have such a lovely family. The fact that you could sing to them is incredible. Whenever I sing to Reuben or Solomon, they most often roll their eyes."

Maria laughed quietly, wishing not to wake up her siblings. From her parents' bedroom she heard her father snoring. This was now time for *herself* to read this letter, this treat she'd been awaiting the whole day. She read the last sentence again, enjoying every word.

> "…whenever I sing to Reuben or Solomon, they most often roll their eyes.
>
> Solomon all the time thinks of Hannah.
>
> And Reuben, too, I bet you, is thinking of some girl as well. I've seen how eager he was to go to the beach and look at all the women there. I told him he should close his mouth so that he won't drool. But he didn't like my comment!"

Maria shook her head, "Helena Helena…!"

> "I like it here. I especially like that my Father

is around more. Back in the city he is busy all the time. Here he reads the newspaper. Sure, don't be mistaken, he did bring with him quite a few folders from the office. But he's also available. Somewhat."

Maria smiled. That's good.

"My mother is the happiest. And so am I."

Maria touched the paper with her finger, over the small stars separating the next paragraph.

"P.S.

I searched for what else to write. I wish I knew what to add! But I see that each day makes the letter older and also further away from you, dearest Maria. So I will let the letter go as it is. This does NOT show my utter appreciation for your kindness to have addressed me here. Please do so again as soon as you receive this letter! I hope that by then I would know what to write to you next time!

Until then, faithfully yours,

Helena Goldstein."

Maria bit her lip. This was wonderful. Just wonderful! She took out her paper and her favorite pen. It was late already, but this was important.

She wanted to write back. Now.

But instead she found herself copying Helena's beautiful signature. Trying, unsuccessfully, to get that twirl, especially around the "H" and the "G". She sighed. She knew she needed to begin writing soon.

CHAPTER 7

"I received another letter! I received another letter!"

Everyone was amused. Helena ran around the house, told her brothers, the servant downstairs and the maids upstairs. She thought of running to the beach and screaming it out loud. But... that, she knew, would be a waste of time.

So she ran into her room, slammed the door, indicating she had some *real* work to do. Staring and sighing at the math assignment could wait

She lay on her stomach on the bed, and eagerly opened the letter.

> "Dearest Helena,
>
> I just now read your letter and I intend on going first thing tomorrow with Eddie and Sashinka to the post office. They will enjoy it.
>
> It's now been ten days since the beginning of summer break, and I dread thinking of the rest. This break is too long. I wish they would

have broken it into smaller breaks throughout the year. Also, this would be so much better for the students as the flow of our education would not stop so abruptly."

Helena shook her head. This was so typical of Maria. "The flow of our education." *Maria Maria!*

"The city feels a little dull. I realize many people have gone out of the city for the summer. Father spoke of busy days at the train station, but now it has eased. At the post office there is no line anymore. Nor is there a line at the grocery store. Also, the vendors seem less enthusiastic to work. It's a pity. Everything happens so slowly.

Sashinka is excited about being the eldest in kindergarten next year. I promised to sew her a bag embroidered with her initials. I hope this will keep me busy for several days. But I desperately think of what to do.

I did take some books from the library. I was the only one in the youth section, could you imagine?"

Helena laughed and exclaimed at the letter, "Of course Maria!"

"Eddie finished his Karl May book, which makes me happy. We'll borrow a new book for him soon, maybe tomorrow. Meantime all he speaks about is Indian chiefs and cowboys, and speaks in tongues and explains it is Indian… he can be so funny…

Do tell me about the sea, and the waves, and

the sound of the seagulls. I would love to explore sea life, see sea stars and seahorses… Do you notice the tides? Does it really change according to the moon? Tell me, please, do not spare your thoughts.

Yours fondly,

Maria Bozek.

P.S.

What do you think of my new signature? Not as beautiful as yours, but I like it better than my old one!"

Helena turned over onto her back and smiled. What a beautiful letter! She looked at it again. Two full pages. She must be able to respond with *at least* that length. She looked at the small handwriting and at the funny looking signature. "Oh Maria!" she laughed.

Helena had never before wanted to return to school as much as she did that year.

"I have a surprise for you!" she whispered into Maria's ear as they hugged when seeing each other for the first time after the long summer.

"And I for you!" Maria whispered back, her eyes shining.

During the long break between classes they ran up to the third floor and quietly climbed out the window onto the roof, each holding a small bag in her hand.

Helena looked at the view. "It's so good to be here again!"

Maria nodded. There was so much she wanted to say.

"I've missed the city," Helena continued, "and I even missed the school!"

Maria smiled.

"Here," Helena said and handed Maria a small brown bag, "I got these for you. But…" she hesitated, "please don't tell Gisele or Isabella or anyone because I didn't—"

"I promise."

Helena then took the brown bag back, "Guess what it is!"

Maria shrugged her shoulders, "I don't know."

"Guess!"

Maria searched for the right guess.

Helena pressed, "Just guess!"

"Helena! I don't know!"

Helena shook the bag in front of Maria's face. It sounded like small stones.

Still, Maria wouldn't guess.

Helena shook her head and handed Maria the bag, "So open it!"

Maria opened the small bag and exclaimed "Helena!"

Seashells in various golden colors filled the bag.

She touched them, caressing the different shapes and sizes. She held them to her nose. "They smell like the sea!"

Helena laughed, "Of course they do!"

Maria inspected them, turning each one, looking at it from every angle. "Wow, Helena, it's *exactly*… it means so *much* to me…"

"Did you see the small bag inside?"

"Small bag?"

Inside the brown bag there was a tiny paper bag.

Helena's smile grew bigger, "Open it!"

Maria opened it. It was a fossil of a…

"No!"

"Yes!"

"No! Is this the tail of a… *seahorse?*"

"Yes Maria! Reuben found it! He said it must be from a tiny seahorse."

"Oh Helena!" Maria said and embraced Helena. "This is…"

"Magical, right?"

"Yes!"

Helena smiled. The schoolyard was busy with students. Gisele and the others would be wondering where she was.

Maria bit her lip. She had also brought Helena a present, but it was nothing in comparison… She sighed, "Helena, I'm afraid this does not match your generous gift…"

Helena tut-tutted, "Don't be silly!"

Maria handed the small brown bag to Helena.

Helena opened it. Inside she saw a small handmade purse. "Oh my!" she exclaimed, "It's beautiful! And it has my initials!"

Maria looked down, "I tried to capture your swirling signature…"

"I love it! This is so much better than my gift!"

Maria shook her head, "Yours is much better. All I did was to sew this together…—"

"Yeah, but you *made* it, Maria. I just *found* these…" She hugged Maria. "Thank you so much!"

The school bell rang.

They crawled carefully back to the window and climbed inside, closing the window behind them and running to class. Each girl hid her precious bag in her hand, protecting it.

She was 25-years-old now. But she looked older. She'd been through so much these past few years. The war. Escaping.

The train, now in her beloved homeland, chugged its way through fields and forests. The announcements in the train were now made in her own language. She missed her language.

She sighed. Somehow she felt safer now, in her

own country.

She opened her valise, which held her only possessions in this world: some clothes, a few letters, a journal and the little brown bag.

She reached in and pulled out the old, time-worn brown bag. It had been folded and unfolded over the years hundreds of times.

She thought of getting rid of it. It was too revealing of her true identity. It could have proved disastrous. It could have cost her her life.

But she kept it.

Carefully opening the brown bag, she took out the tiny purse. Tears stung her eyes.

She had not allowed herself to cry for so many years. But now the tears filled her eyes as her fingers caressed the embroidered letters.

"H. G."

CHAPTER 8

Not long after the school year began, Helena invited Maria to come to the synagogue with her. "It's a special day for us, I think you'd like it."

Maria asked her parents. Whilst her mother did not want her gone for too long, her father insisted that she should go.

Helena was in heaven to hear the good news. "We'll have so much fun together! It's always so boring for me alone..."

Maria was excited. "Do I need to bring anything?"

"No, just come dressed in white."

"In white?"

Helena nodded.

As they approached the building, Maria was amazed to see everyone was wearing white: men, women and even the children.

They climbed the stairs following Mrs. Goldstein to the second floor of the large synagogue. Helena whispered to Maria, "We call it the Day of Atonement. We need to atone and ask for forgiveness for our sins, I think…."

They sat down on the wooden benches, looking at the grandeur below. Maria liked the stained glass windows. It looked like a church, but… whiter. Especially with all the people wearing white.

Helena whispered to her, "It goes on like this for hours, sitting, standing. It can be very boring…"

But Maria found none of it boring. The men downstairs were moving and nodding their heads incessantly. And many women upstairs, around Maria, did so as well. She watched with fascination how the women moved their lip rapidly, as if under a trance.

But what moved her most of all was when people began crying. Real crying, when the lead man (Helena called him the 'cantor') sang with a deep voice, looking up to the ceiling, and the entire synagogue shook with the power of his voice.

Even Helena's mother had tears in her eyes.

Maria couldn't stop herself from asking Helena, whispering ever so quietly, "What is he *saying?*"

Helena grimaced, "I'm not quite sure… I'm not sure anyone here understands really…"

The following day, Helena did not attend school. It

was a day of fasting for her. Nearly half the class did not come to school that day. And a few teachers were missing too.

But the day after, the whole class returned, and life continued as usual. Mr. Kissinger spoke monotonously while most students didn't follow. Mrs. Schlesinger was in love with the current poet they were studying. And the new history teacher spoke about the Great War with fervor.

CHAPTER 9

Winter approached, and the streets were decorated for Christmas. In the schoolyard Roman boasted to the girls how he and his father had gone to the forest and cut down a *huge* tree to place in their house for the holiday.

When he was gone, Helena lamented to Gisele, "I wish we could celebrate Christmas as well."

Maria, sitting next to them, reading a book, tilted her head and listened.

Gisele shrugged her shoulders, "But they don't get to light the candelabrum and eat our great food…"

"Yeah, I know," Helena lamented, "but, you know, Christmas is so festive…."

Maria's eyes widened. She thought it impossible for someone not to celebrate Christmas. It was the best thing about the winter!

Two days later, during history lesson, Maria wrote down: "Do you want to come and celebrate Christmas at my house?"

Helena squinted at the note, her eyes growing large with disbelief. She quickly wrote "Really???"

Maria smiled and wrote, "YES!"

Helena's eyes glittered. "But," she wrote, "your parents…???"

"My mother," Maria wrote, "invited you."

"That can't be!!!" Helena wrote.

Maria smiled and wrote, "But it's true!"

Helena grinned. She couldn't believe it.

Maria ran to the door, "I'll get it!"

Mrs. Bozek hurried to walk to the door from the kitchen, and shouted at her husband sitting in the living room, "Come now!"

Maria opened the door and exclaimed, "Helena!"

Helena stood at the door, wearing her new fur coat and carrying a suitcase. Mr. Goldstein was standing behind her in the snowy street.

Eddie and Sashinka hurried to join and hide behind their parents.

Mrs. Bozek hurried to say, "Well come in already Helena, don't stand there outside!"

Helena walked in.

Mr. Goldstein raised his hand, "Thank you. Merry Christmas!"

Mr. Bozek raised his hand as well, "Happy holidays! Why won't you come in for a moment, have something warm to drink? Make a toast?"

Mr. Goldstein waved his hand, pointing at the direction of the tram. "My wife…"

Mr. Bozek gestured knowingly, 'Of course!' and nodded his head.

Mr. Goldstein tipped his hat and walked away.

Mr. Bozek closed the door and headed back to the living room. Mrs. Bozek was already back in the kitchen. Helena and Maria remained at the entrance, jumping in each other's arms. "I can't believe I'm here!"

"I can't believe you're here!"

"Girls," Mrs. Bozek shouted, "enough with that. Maria, take Helena's coat already!"

"Yes Mama!"

Helena whispered, "It's okay," and took her coat off, placing it on the hanger.

Maria whispered, "What's with the suitcase?"

Helena's eyes glittered, "Well, my night clothes and all, but also," she whispered, "presents for Eddie and Sashinka!"

Maria shook her head, "You shouldn't have!"

"I wanted to!"

Eddie and Sashinka were now in the living room,

playing. Helena entered the living room and gasped, "Wow! What a beautiful tree! And what a huge table! Where are the beds?"

Maria's mother came out of the kitchen, beaming, "Beautiful, right?"

Helena nodded, and Eddie and Sashinka hurried to show her the decorations they made for the tree.

Helena smiled, "Wow, you did that Eddie? The star?"

Maria smiled at her.

Helena then looked at the large table with chairs and plates already set up. There was a white tablecloth, but there seemed to be hay all around. They must still need to do some final cleaning, she thought.

Maria looked at her with joy and whispered, "The table – it's made of two beds put together!"

"No!" Helena motioned with her mouth.

"Yes! My father put a big wooden board on the two beds, see?" She moved the large tablecloth.

"Brilliant!" Helena whispered. She smiled at Mr. Bozek, who was reading the newspaper.

Mrs. Bozek shouted from the kitchen, "Maria, I need you!"

Maria walked to the kitchen, and Helena followed her, saying, "I can help too!"

Mrs. Bozek waved her hand, "You are our guest! Now go to the living room and leave us alone. I need to concentrate!"

Maria smiled at Helena. Helena smiled back and went to the living room to play with the younger children.

A few minutes later the grandparents arrived. Helena was introduced to them. They were Mrs. Bozek's parents, and were much younger than Helena's grandparents. They sat in the living room and the grandfather began to have a long conversation with Mr. Bozek; the two laughed together amiably. The grandmother tried to help in the kitchen but was soon shooed away by Mrs. Bozek, "Mother, don't disturb me," she exclaimed.

The grandmother then came to the living room and played for a while with the grandchildren.

Soon, the doorbell rang again. This time it was Mr. Bozek's parents. They looked much older. In fact, Helena thought, that the grandfather looked quite ancient.

The small living room was packed. Helena tried to fit in, but really hoped Maria would come out of the kitchen.

Eddie was running to the window every minute or so, exclaiming, "I don't see it yet Papa! I don't see it yet!"

Mr. Bozek kept talking with his father in law. The other grandfather soon fell asleep on his wife's shoulder.

Then, Eddie exclaimed from near the window, "I see it Papa! The first star!"

Mr. Bozek walked to the window. "Indeed."

As if waiting for that moment, Mrs. Bozek ran out of the kitchen, snatching off her apron, "Very good. Now sit down everybody! I don't want the food to get cold!"

Everyone sat down quickly.

Silence ensued.

Mrs. Bozek elbowed her husband, who coughed, "Papa!"

The old and feeble grandfather seemed to be awoken from a daze, "Yes?"

"The prayer, Papa!"

"Why of course," said the puzzled grandfather, and the children burst into laughter. Mrs. Bozek silenced them at once.

The old grandfather joined his hands with his wife and the other grandfather, and soon everyone was holding hands. Helena held Maria's and Eddie's hands. She found it quite weird. They each held their hands very tightly.

The old grandfather said a prayer, and they all said "Amen" and crossed themselves. Helena did not, hoping no one had noticed.

Then Eddie exclaimed with excitement, "The Christmas wafer!"

The old grandfather took the large piece of unleavened wafer at the center of the table, and broke it into two pieces. He looked at his wife and said, "Merry Christmas!"

He then turned to the other grandfather and said,

"Merry Christmas." He handed them the broken pieces of wafer, and soon they began passing and breaking the wafers to others, blessing everyone with Merry Christmas and other wishes.

Maria handed her a small piece of wafer and smiled, shyly, "Merry Christmas Helena!"

Helena smiled, "Merry Christmas Maria!"

Helena also received a small piece from Eddie, and to her surprise everyone kept chopping their pieces of wafer and passing from one to the other, exclaiming "Good year!" and "Health and prosperity" among other blessings.

Then everyone ate their wafers and crumbs. Helena thought it was so peculiar!

Maria's mother left the table, and Maria hurried to follow her. Helena noticed there was something tilting the plate under her plate—no, under the tablecloth—and quietly sneaked her hand under the tablecloth to remove some… hay?

"Father," Eddie said, "she's removing the hay!"

Helena's face reddened at once. Was she not supposed to…—

Maria, serving the first bowls of red beetroot soup smiled and whispered, "It's tradition to place hay under the table and under the tablecloth."

Helena mumbled, "Of… of course…" She was determined not to move or do anything else that would attract attention.

But the old grandmother smiled at her from across the table, "It's to remember that Jesus was born and put in a *manger*, you see?"

Helena mumbled, "Of course…"

Luckily, Maria's father changed the subject, "Tell us, Eddie, what have you been studying in school…"

When the soup was served, Maria sat down and noticed Helena's red face. She smiled, "Is everything okay?"

Helena whispered, placing her hands on her hot cheeks, "Why? Do I look redder than the soup?"

Maria grinned and said reassuringly, "It's so great to have you here!"

The evening continued with more and more food. The tiny kitchen kept producing dishes heaped with rollmops, cabbage rolls, cooked mushrooms, dumplings filled with cheese and potatoes, stewed sauerkraut, many kinds of salads, and many kinds of fish.

Mrs. Bozek looked at Helena, "There is no meat here, only fish, so eat!"

Helena looked at her, puzzled.

"I went to the market," Mrs. Bozek said, "and asked what you *cannot* eat, but I understood fish always works, right?"

Helena nodded.

"Well, eat everything then!"

Maria, feeling a little guilty, whispered to Helena,

"It's our tradition that you have to eat all twelve dishes."

Hearing her, Mr. Bozek added, "Because of the twelve months of the year. It's for you to have a good year!"

"Fool," Mrs. Bozek retorted, "it's because of the twelve *apostles!*"

"Well I heard it was the twelve months of the year!"

"Who," Maria jumped, "who… wants *kompot?*"

Everyone cheered, and so Maria hurried to fetch the pitchers of the sweet beverage from the kitchen. Helena, seeing that Mrs. Bozek was sitting, got up to help Maria, and looked at Mrs. Bozek worriedly, fearing she would scold her. But she was busy eating and talking to the grandmother.

In the small kitchen, Maria smiled at Helena, "Is everything okay?"

Helena, still red and quite embarrassed, said a little too eagerly, "Yes! It's so… *lively!*"

Maria smiled, took one pitcher and pointed at the second pitcher, and Helena carried it and followed her to the living room.

They poured kompot for everyone. When Helena poured some kompot for Mrs. Bozek, she was surprised to see Maria's mother looking at her and nodding, "You're a good girl, Helena."

This made Helena feel much better. But this was not to last for long.

After all the poppy seed cakes were eaten, the dried apples and plums were finished, and all the small sweets were tasted, Helena helped Mrs. Bozek and Maria take the dishes to the kitchen. All the while Eddie kept nagging, "Now, Papa? *Now?*"

Mr. Bozek did not respond, and kept talking to his father-in-law. Eventually he said to Eddie, "When your mama says!"

When the table was finally clean Mrs. Bozek said, "We can now move to the tree."

Eddie and Sashinka cheered. Everyone carried their chairs to the tree, and Mr. Bozek, with the help of his father-in-law, pushed the table-made-of-beds to the corner of the room.

Helena hurried to her suitcase. She opened it and excitedly took the two large packages out. She placed them under the tree along with the other presents, and asked Maria, who came and sat down, "Is it okay where I put them?"

Maria smiled and nodded.

The old grandfather once again fell asleep on the old grandmother's shoulder. Eddie and Sashinka were ecstatic. Mrs. Bozek sat near the tree, and Mr. Bozek stood behind her, massaging her shoulders. This was a little embarrassing for Helena to watch.

Mrs. Bozek then cleared her throat, "First, Sashinka will open her present."

Little Sasha eagerly took her gift from under the

tree, and tore the wrapping paper apart.

Maria smiled at Helena.

Sashinka discovered a white dress, perfect for her size. "Mama, Papa!" She exclaimed.

Maria said to her, "Now kiss Mama and Papa!"

Sasha kissed them. Mrs. Bozek said, "It's from your grandparents too. Go kiss them too!"

After Sashinka finished the round of kisses, Eddie shouted, "Now it's my turn!"

Mrs. Bozek said, "Now you Eddie."

He opened his gift. It was a small train, made out of wood, painted in red. He thanked his parents and kissed them, and then kissed the grandparents.

Then came Maria's turn. She opened her package. "New notebooks!" she exclaimed.

Helena smiled. She was a little disappointed for Maria.

"Look inside," Mrs. Bozek said proudly, "with a set of pens! Like those you like!"

"Mama! Thank you!" Maria kissed her mother, "Papa!" she kissed him as well. She went around and kissed the four grandparents. She then said excitedly, "But... there are two more packages! Let's guess who they are for?"

Sasha and Eddie began screaming, "Me! Me!"

Maria looked at Helena, who whispered, "The red for Sasha, the blue for Eddie."

"Go ahead Sashinka," Maria said and pointed at

the large red gift.

Sashinka opened it eagerly. It was a beautiful doll, with a dress and a brown hair, braided into two braids. Sashinka couldn't hold her excitement, "Is this for me? Really? Really?!"

She jumped around and ran with the doll. Maria laughed, "Now kiss Helena!"

Helena leaned down as Sashinka kissed her shyly. Helena looked at Mrs. Bozek, who did not seem overly pleased for some reason.

Then Eddie exclaimed, "My turn, my turn!"

He waited for his mother's nodding approval, and then opened the large package. "Wow!!!" he screamed. "A train! A mechanical train!"

Helena smiled. Then, her smile disappeared instantly as Eddie screamed, "This is so much better than the wooden one!"

Mrs. Bozek got up at once, "Come, Maria! We need to clean the dishes!"

It all happened very fast. Maria gave Helena a sorry look, and she disappeared. There was a long silence in the living room, as if Helena had done something awful. The only one speaking was Eddie, who was running the train around, looking at its intricate wheels, rocking levers and the various springs.

Mr. Bozek was the first to speak. "Well! Let's… sing a little!" He got up and brought out a guitar. He began singing, and the grandparents joined him.

Helena knew the song, and in different

circumstances would have began singing with her beautiful soprano. But now she stared down at the floor and tried to smile at the excited two kids with their gifts.

She wanted so badly to go and see Maria in the kitchen, help her, speak to her, hear from her that she just imagined, and that she hadn't done something unforgivable....

But Maria was gone. Mr. Bozek tried cheering the atmosphere, but Helena felt stupid. Stupid, stupid, stupid! She shouldn't have brought such expensive gifts! Tears welled in her eyes, and she got up and ran to the back door. She exited the house and entered the small bathroom hut in the backyard.

She stood there, in the cold and smelly bathroom, for what seemed like forever, cursing herself, crying, wanting to go home so badly.

"Helena? Helena is everything okay?"

Helena heard Maria's voice, wiped her tears and shouted over the door of the bathroom hut, "Sure…"

"Helena, did you *cry?*"

"No…!"

"Helena, open the door for me!"

Helena opened the door. Maria looked at Helena's puffy face. She reached her hands to hug her, "Come here!"

Helena hugged her. "I feel like a *fool*, I didn't mean to…"

"Enough with that, all is well! Did you see how Eddie liked your gift—"

"But your mama…"

"My mother can sometimes be… You'll see, tomorrow she'll be hailing your generous gifts…!"

"No she won't!"

Maria grabbed Helena's arms, "Listen to me, Helena! You are *so* kind, you've been *so* kind. You should be *proud* of yourself for being so… *generous*…! Helena!"

Helena sniffled and nodded.

"Now," Maria said, "in a moment we'll go inside where it's warm, and you'll join us for the singing… I want the little ones to hear you sing! And then we'll go to the midnight mass. Were you ever at the midnight mass?"

Helena shook her head 'no' and wiped her cheeks again.

Maria smiled, "You'll *love* it!" She hugged Helena again, "I am so happy you are here!"

"You *are?*" Helena murmured, "Didn't I embarrass you…?"

From inside the house they heard singing. Maria said, "Of course not! And I'm so happy you are here with us! Now come, let's go inside."

Helena nodded. All she wanted was to go *home*. But she was a big girl now. What would Reuben and

Solomon say if she suddenly returned back home?

'No', she thought to herself. She was strong. She'll stay.

She'll even have fun.

Maria looked at her. "Ready?"

Helena nodded.

They walked inside.

CHAPTER 10

Spring came. And in Helena's house everyone was preparing for the big Passover dinner.

Helena made sure that everyone in the household wouldn't say or do anything embarrassing during the big dinner. She was so excited about Maria coming and sleeping over for the first time. But she was also nervous.

Memories from her uncomfortable visit at Maria's during Christmas made her extra cautious about Maria's visit. Helena knew that her uncle, Bernie, could be rather foolish and inappropriate, and so she asked her mother to speak to him in advance. She wanted no embarrassments. No chagrins. No exasperating moments. She wanted Maria to feel like a part of the family. Welcomed.

Maria fit in perfectly at the dinner table. She was pleasant, cordial, and smiled politely to everyone: Maria's parents, her two brothers, her four grandparents, her uncle and aunt and their two cousins.

Everyone seemed to like her. Helena was so pleased. As the long and arduous ceremony continued, she prayed that it would soon finish without any incidents.

But then it came.

Helena watched it happen. She saw uncle Bernie as he looked at Maria a little too intently.

He snorted at her loudly, "Aren't you *afraid*, little girl, that we will *cook* you tonight and drink your *blood?*"

Mrs. Goldstein exclaimed, "Bernie!"

His wife, aunt Goldie, buried her face in her hands, "Bernie!"

Helena was *mortified.*

But Maria didn't miss a bit, "No, sir. And Helena had already warned me about you!"

Everyone laughed, and Helena, who stopped breathing, now breathed in deeply. Mrs. Goldstein said, "Well done, Helena, for warning Maria. And well done, Maria, for listening. My brother Bernie can be rather nonsensical!"

Uncle Bernie smiled lovingly and nodded.

This was not it, though. When the ceremony was about to end, Helena's grandfather stood and began an emotional speech, which Helena found quite embarrassing, about the "enemies of the people", and how in each generation someone comes to "kill us all". He exclaimed, "And now we should not be afraid of this lunatic...!"

Maria looked at Helena and whispered, "Who is he talking about?"

Helena shrugged her shoulders and whispered, "I think he's talking about this nationalist fella who was just elected somewhere... My father and brothers have been arguing about him... but I'm not sure..."

The grandfather continued for what seemed like eternity to Helena, passionately talking in his hoarse voice about how "this *lunatic* won't succeed where *Pharaoh* failed!" and how all will be well, "...as long as we put the *family* above all!"

Mrs. Goldstein hurried to use his dramatic pause and chimed, "Well said, Dad. They tried to kill us, we survived, now let's eat!"

Everyone clapped as the grandfather finally sat down. Helena whispered, "Phew! What a speech!"

Maria smiled. She actually enjoyed the passionate speech. She whispered to Helena, "My grandpa, had he needed to give this speech, would have probably fallen asleep in the middle!"

They smiled at each other.

Maria loved all the various foods. But more so, she loved how after the dinner they were all looking for the hidden flatbread which the grandmother hid somewhere around the house. Helena and Maria looked for it like mad, and so did Reuben and

Solomon and the two cousins.

From the library, Maria called to Helena, who was searching the pantry, "Is it, Helena, wrapped in a white towel?"

"Yes! Did you…?"

Maria came with the towel, wrapping the flatbread, "I'm not sure…?"

"Everyone!" Helena jumped, "Maria found the hidden Afikoman!" Helena ran to the living room where everyone was resting after the meal, "Maria found the Afikoman!"

The grandfather leaned forward and exclaimed, "Very well!"

Maria looked at everyone staring at her.

Helena clapped her hands, "You get to ask for a *prize!*"

Maria reddened, "A prize? I don't…"

Everyone looked at her.

Maria looked down, "I don't…" she shrugged her shoulders, "Just *being* here is a prize…"

Everyone clapped, "Well said!"

The grandmother exclaimed, "Helena! What a good friend you've got!"

Helena beamed.

Helena's grandfather said, "But that won't do. You need to choose something, anything!"

Mrs. Goldstein hurried to say, "Leave her alone.

It's okay, darling," she said to Maria, "you can decide later. Now, everyone, let's sing some of the oldies… Bernie…?"

CHAPTER 11

It took three weeks of pleading.

"But mama!" Maria cried, "It's not charity!"

"Even if it's not, I'm not going to let you go away for a whole week! What will I do with Eddie and Sashinka?"

"Mrs. Szymborska said she'd help with them!"

"Well you know what I think of Mrs. Szymborska!"

"Mom," Maria cried, "I really want to go, I've never been to the sea!"

"So what?! I've also never been, and do you see me crying?"

At school, Helena gave Maria *all* the methods. Whenever Maria gave up, Helena came up with a new plan. Maria would memorize it, but she didn't have much faith in any of Helena's weird ideas.

"Mama," Maria tried one of them, "I promised Helena I'll help her with the *summer math assignment*. Last year she couldn't do it, and she asked me to—"

"Isn't her father an accountant? He can help her!"

"But we also told Mr. Kissinger we'd do the summer biology experiment at the sea, with barnacles and seaweed, he already approved the experiment for us!"

"Oh leave me alone Maria will you!"

Helena kept searching for more ideas. Finally, she decided to involve her mother.

Mrs. Goldstein came one day to pick Helena up from Maria's. "Mrs. Bozek," she said in the living room, "can I have a moment with you?"

"I'm here, am I not?" Mrs. Bozek said.

Mrs. Goldstein smiled to Helena, who, along with Maria, took Eddie and Sasha to play outside.

Helena's heart beat fast. "You'll see," she told Maria outside as they were throwing the ball among the four of them, "my mother will make it happen."

Thirty minutes later Mrs. Goldstein came out the house, smiling. "She'll think on it," she said to Helena. "Now say goodbye to Maria and the siblings and let's hurry, we don't want to be late to the ballet."

It was unclear what was said in the living room, but, miraculously enough, it worked. On July first, boarding the train for the full-day journey toward the country's seaside, was, in addition to the usual yearly quintet of Mr. and Mrs. Goldstein, their two sons and their daughter, also the daughter's best friend: Maria Bozek.

Maria's father, who worked at that very train station, climbed on the train to bid them all farewell, wearing his train engineer's uniform. Mr. Goldstein reassured him, "Don't worry, Mr. Bozek, Maria will be safe with us."

"It's not me who's worried. It's her mother. As for me," Mr. Bozek said and winked at Maria, "I'm just jealous!"

Maria laughed. Helena hurried to say, "Perhaps next time the whole family could come?"

Mr. Bozek smiled, "Whatever God wills." He looked at Mr. and Mrs. Goldstein and tipped his hat at them, "Have a pleasant journey!"

He then got off the train, and tapped the train's conductor on the back, "Take care of them, my daughter is there!"

Maria looked eagerly through the window. "I can't believe we'll spend four full days together!"

Helena jumped, "Right?! Oh I have to take you to the deserted house on the hilltop, if it's still there. Oh, and to the ice-cream parlor, you'll love it…"

"But we must leave time for the biology assignment," Maria added.

"Right." Helena smiled. "Plenty of time!"

It's hard to point out a person's happiest moments in life. Most of the moments of our lives blend together. But those four days on the beach were, for both Maria and Helena, some of the most memorable moments in their lifetime: how Mrs. Goldstein bought the two of them matching bathing suits and Helena cheered ("Don't you just love the belt Maria?"); how they ran up the hill to the deserted house and hid and scared one another (given Helena's many times there with her brothers, she was already a pro); how they ate ice-cream trying *all* the different flavors (until they got sick); how they sunbathed on the beach for hours (and Helena cursed each cloud that hid the sun); how Maria tried learning a few ballet moves from Helena (without much success but with tons of laughter); how they gossiped on the beach about Reuben and Solomon ("I can't *believe* you think Reuben is handsome!"); how they giggled into the night, chattering about Alexander, Roman, and the other boys in class (rating them according to new categories they came up with); how they took pictures with Reuben's new camera and made funny poses (which Helena masterfully directed) and how they took the biology sampling of barnacles' level of acidity and alkalinity in the tide pools (that is, *Maria* took the sampling while Helena mostly chattered).

When the four days were over, they cried in each other's arms at the train station.

Solomon was with them, taking the trip back in order to help in his father's accounting firm for a few weeks, or, according to Helena, to spend time with his darling Hannah. He was also to escort young Maria to the doorstep of her house, as Mrs. Goldstein promised Mrs. Bozek.

Helena cried to Maria, "Promise you'll write to me as soon as you enter your house!"

"I promise. Promise you'll look into the math assignment, a little each day!"

"I promise."

They hugged and whispered, "Friends forever."

"Forever!"

Solomon coughed. "Shall we?"

Helena nodded.

Maria climbed with him onto the train, "I'll write as soon as I get home! Please thank your parents again!"

Helena walked on the platform, following them as they took their seats. They waved goodbye to one another on both sides of the window. The conductor blew the whistle. The doors closed.

Helena motioned with her lip, "I'll miss you!"

"I'll miss you too!"

The train began moving. They waved to each other. Helena kept waving on the platform as the train left, leaving a trail of smoke above the platform as it slowly disappeared in the horizon.

PART TWO

Based on a true story

CHAPTER 12

The years passed.

An older Maria and an older Helena now sat at the front of the class.

Over the years their friendship had only grown stronger.

Maria often spent holiday evenings with Helena's family, learning of their intricate traditions, deeds, and unique humor. Helena, too, didn't miss an opportunity to be with the Bozeks. She learned to develop thick skin with Mrs. Bozek, learning that ultimately the matron only had good intentions. When they held hands before each meal, she prayed with them too. When they crossed their chests, she looked down and waited for them to finish.

But apart from such minute differences, they were like sisters.

They had their ups and downs, too, like sisters.

Helena was very much interested in boys, while Maria was always more reticent about the subject.

Helena sometimes scolded Maria, explaining to her that life "isn't all about books and exams!"

But Maria didn't spare Helena from her reprimands either, explaining to her, like she were a child, that she must "invest time in studying," and that "grades do matter!"

Oddly enough, they slowly became more similar. Helena began to find some pleasure in numbers, especially when it came to money. Maria began to find pleasure in social circumstances. She was still very quiet, but some of the freedom she learned from Helena began showing up in social situations.

The other students referred to them as "Helena and Maria." Helena's name did come *first*, but Maria's name was never forgotten. They were invited together to parties. They were always seated together when going to a café or to a performance.

They sometimes even completed each other's sentences, bursting into laughter, leaving everyone else a little envious of their close bond.

However, while their relationship seemed never to be broken, the safe world around them began to crack.

The army recruited many young men, trying to prepare for a severe blow from the growing army-nation across borders.

But the army, as much as it tried, soon lost to a brutal attack. Now, the new occupying army was beginning to change things.

It started with laws that at first seem trivial, such as not allowing people of a certain heritage to wear fur, for example.

Then, large businesses, some of which were owned by members of Helena's extended family, were confiscated and nationalized.

Helena and Maria were not too worried. They were excited to finish school and begin university together, making sure they were both going to the same university. They fretted for months about what to study.

Helena thought of following the footsteps of her brothers.

"But Helena," Maria retorted, "*accounting?* Seriously? I cannot see you possibly…—"

"Look," Helena sighed, "it's a good profession. It's a *stable* profession…"

"You sound just like Mr. Goldstein!"

Helena tried to smile, "Well, I guess, there's acting in it *too*, you see? With large clients one must know how to present and convince… And being a *woman* accountant is quite a big thing, Maria, there aren't many, and I can change that…"

Maria sighed. "I'm not sure you'll be happy…"

"Well," Helena said, calculating her words, "it is a *needed* profession. And now with the *war* and with things changing like that…"

Maria understood that reasoning. The Goldsteins

now moved from their large house into a smaller apartment, trying to save money and assets as much as possible. She could understand Helena, to an extent.

"And you?" Helena asked, "Are you sure about pharmaceutical sciences?"

Maria's eyes glowed, "It's the closest thing to being a doctor, you know, and I hope to help people that way…"

Helena smiled, "One day you'll invent the cure for some big disease, and you'll be world famous!"

Maria laughed, "If anyone will be famous out of the two of us, it'll be you!"

The atmosphere at university was different than in high school. Sure, it was larger. But that was not it. There were some people who were adamant that Helena and people of her heritage should not be admitted into universities.

Maria argued with one of the new friends on campus, "Of course they should be admitted! And to *all* universities!"

"Are you one of *them* or what?" the friend retorted, "Besides, there isn't enough space in all of the academies for all of those who seek higher education, so it's only reasonable…"

Maria tried arguing, but she slowly saw how the army's radio, the pamphlets and the posters were being successful in changing people's thoughts.

People changed. Even people from her old class.

One day she met her old friend Alexander on the street. She hadn't seen him for over a year. They spoke for several minutes. He then asked, "Are you still a friend of Helena?"

"Of course! Why shouldn't I be?"

Alexander looked around. "Well, it's not very *wise*, you know…"

At home, Maria shared her frustration with her parents and siblings. Eddie was now in high school, and Sasha was soon finishing elementary school. Maria complained all the time, "I just can't understand people's idiocy!"

But things were tense at home as well. Her mother was laid off from her work in the factory as the occupying army was bringing its "own" people. Unemployment of factory workers was high due to the occupation of the new workforce. But Maria's beloved country was now carrying the burden.

Her mother ceaselessly looked for a job, but to no avail. In the meantime, she was cleaning houses when she could, but the demand for cleaning ladies and maids was not high.

They were all now dependent on Maria's father's income. The occupying army had fired many of the train's workers. There was a danger of Mr. Bozek being fired as well.

At the dinner table, Maria was exasperated. "I just can't stand seeing how people fall into this talk of hatred…"

Eddie, who was usually quiet by the dinner table, said, "But there is *some* truth to it, isn't there? What about that corrupt minister? He was one of *them.*"

Mr. Bozek suddenly slammed his fist on the table. They were all startled. "I will not," he muttered through his teeth, "let you... speak this way... in my household!"

Eddie looked down.

Mrs. Bozek went to the stove to get more potatoes.

"Father," said Maria, "there's no need to—"

"What do you even know, Eddie," Mr. Bozek stood up, pushing his plate, "what do you even know about that minister, huh? Don't believe everything you hear, son. I think it was a set up!"

Eddie sighed, "But Father, they found..."

"I'll have none of it!"

"Now-now," Mrs. Bozek said, "we should all finish eating. Sashinka, how was school? You had an exam, didn't you?"

"Yes Mama. It went well."

"Good," Mrs. Bozek said and tried to smile.

Silence ensued. All eyes were fixed on plates.

One morning, as Maria left the house to university, she saw large posters affixed to walls everywhere. Reading it, her heart sank.

She hurried to the accounting studies faculty to find Helena. But she wasn't there. No one had seen her.

Maria uncharacteristically decided to skip university. She took the tram to the Goldstein's apartment.

As she climbed the stairs, she heard noise behind the door. They were talking and arguing. She rang the bell.

Silence ensued inside.

"It's me!" Maria called, "Maria, for Helena!"

"Maria!" Mrs. Goldstein opened the door.

Maria looked at them. Helena was there, along with Mr. Goldstein, Reuben, Solomon, and Solomon's fiancée Hannah. Helena came over and hugged her. Her eyes were worried.

"Have you all," Maria asked, "seen the signs?"

They nodded.

Helena sighed and walked over to the sofa. Maria followed her and sat down next to her, holding her hand.

Mr. Goldstein looked tired. Maria realized how old he had become. He looked at Mrs. Goldstein. "I'm not leaving my parents! If your brother wants to go, let him go."

Mrs. Goldstein fidgeted with her hands. "Bernie says nothing good will come out of it. And that the war won't be over any time soon. The occupying army, he said, is only advancing..."

Maria murmured, "My father says the same."

Everyone looked at her. She nodded, "He's been saying how the army is only sending more and more soldiers and equipment on the tracks all the time, advancing east and south."

Mr. Goldstein sighed. "This too shall pass."

Maria looked worriedly at Helena. Helena's eyes looked somewhat hollow. "You all," Maria said slowly, "should not move into the enclosure. I don't feel good about it."

Solomon walked around the room. "Me neither. Father, it's insane! Now this enclosure, then what?"

Mr. Goldstein sighed. "Bernie said he's unable to procure any permits for my parents or," his voice grew stronger as he looked at Mrs. Goldstein, "or for your parents. I'm not leaving *anyone* behind! We are together in this!"

Solomon stormed out of the room. Hannah got up and joined him in the other room.

Maria realized she walked into a sensitive situation. What would she have done had she been in their position?

CHAPTER 13

After the Goldsteins moved into the enclosed neighborhood, the streets of that neighborhood were soon surrounded by a fence. Maria tried to convince the soldiers at the entrance several times, with various pretenses, to let her in. But they never did.

Nor was she able to give a letter to anyone. All of the residents of the enclosure were now to wear an armband indicating their lower status. And if they were caught outside the enclosure or near the fence speaking to anybody, the punishment was death without trial.

"I can't stand it!" Maria said one evening at the dinner table.

The family dinners had become quieter. Mr. Bozek became more agitated, and no one wanted to make him upset.

Maria continued, "I must know how Helena is

doing. It's springtime, that's when they celebrate Passover…"

Quiet ensued.

Then Eddie spoke, "I heard of a boy from school who manages to get things across."

Maria looked at him, "Do you? Eddie! Why didn't you tell me?!"

"I just found out today," Eddie said sheepishly, "He has a friend from the enclosure, who works outside. He has a permit, and he sneaks things in."

Maria stood up, "I'm going to write her a letter right now."

Mrs. Bozek said, "Right now you'll finish your dinner…—"

Mr. Bozek put his hand on his wife's hand.

Maria went to the living room and began writing.

The response Maria received three days later was laconic.

"Dearest M.

Your letter brought a ray of light into my day.

I think of our days on the beach often. Also, of the fun we had.

I wish I could see you soon. I hope the war will be over soon.

H."

Maria read it again and again, not understanding. Why was Helena not writing *more?* This was so odd! Was there some sort of code in her words?

She read the short letter again and again. She was puzzled. Did she do anything that might have offended Helena? Why was Helena so brief?

Was she in a danger? Was she upset with her?

These thoughts tortured her. She found it hard to concentrate in university. All of the chemistry lessons blurred together. She found none of it important. None of it made sense.

One day, while she was in class, she heard shouting in the distance, and some gun shots.

What was going on?!

Two days later, Eddie brought home a letter.

"Dearest Maria,"

Maria looked at the short letter, her hands trembling.

> "They took my father, and many of the men in the enclosure, to a work camp. The soldiers didn't say where it is.
>
> My mother is going crazy with worry.
>
> Could you please find out where this camp is? I was wondering whether your Father could find out somehow at the train station…? I hope it's not too much to ask. It will mean

the world for me to know where the work camp is.

I hope I have not offended you in any way. You are always in my heart.

H."

The following evening Maria's father did not return home for dinner.

Maria was upset, "Why is he taking his time? He promised he'd find out and tell me. Where is he?"

"Hush now," Mrs. Bozek said. Her husband was over an hour late. "We'll begin eating. Eddie, do you want to lead the prayer?"

Then they all ate quietly. Maria jumped out of her seat at each noise, hoping it was her father at the door. She needed to know where that camp was so she could write Helena and have it sent to her first thing in the morning with Eddie's friend. The thought of Mrs. Goldstein's pain bothered her tremendously.

She waited and waited.

At eleven o'clock at night the key was finally heard in the door.

Maria, studying her pharmaceutical textbooks in the kitchen, jumped to the door.

She was disgusted. Her father smelled like alcohol. "Father!" she scolded him, whispering as to not to wake up Eddie and Sasha, "I've been waiting for you!"

"Move aside…!"

Her father barely made his way into the house. He was very drunk. Maria had never seen him that way.

Mrs. Bozek stood at the end of the hall. He walked toward her and fell into her arms. She took him into their bedroom and closed the door.

Maria was shocked. What was going on? She knocked on her parent's door.

"Leave me alone…!" her father groaned from the bedroom.

Maria opened the door and closed it behind her.

Her mother looked at her, worried.

Maria swallowed her saliva. Her father was laying on his back on the bed. His eyes were staring at the ceiling.

"Father! I've asked you to find out…—"

"Can't you," he muttered, "just leave me alone?!"

Maria's chin began quivering. Her mother looked at her, her eyes wide open, saying nothing.

"Father?" Maria said, "what did you…?"

Her father shrieked. He began crying.

She had never seen him cry before.

"The trains," he muttered, "they go into the

forests full, but they…"

Silence followed.

He stared at the ceiling. "They… come back empty."

CHAPTER 14

How the years had passed. The train proceeded quickly toward her beloved city. She watched as the landscape changed in front of her.

Home.

It was home. She remembered these views from her childhood.

She did not want to think about what happened.

She sighed. Can one just erase certain events from one's mind?

She remembered how she and Maria, so many years before, sat on the beach, writing things in the sand. Then the sea would come and wash them away.

Could she just magically erase some of her memories?

She wanted to so badly.

She looked at the views. Spring was here. Things were blooming.

Blooming. As if Mother Nature was unaware of

these past years of the war. As if she didn't hear what happened. As if nothing had happened.

She looked at the forest through her window. She remembered how she and Maria used to run in the trees.

Would she ever be able to be so carefree again?

CHAPTER 15

After the transport that took Helena's father away, there was another.

Eddie's friend, no longer had his acquaintance that could smuggle letters in and out.

Maria asked around. But it was dangerous to ask around.

You never knew who was listening, who could report.

Friends became enemies. Enemies disguised themselves as friends.

One day in university she spotted Roman. She remembered how at the end of high school he used to date one girl. She was one of *them,* wasn't she? Perhaps he could pass a letter to Helena?

Maria took Roman aside, trying to read his eyes. Was he now brainwashed as well?

How could she ask him?

He looked back at her. "How have you been

doing, Maria?"

She looked at his eyes. "Roman, can I trust you?"

He smiled. "You'll have to trust yourself first."

"Do you…" she hesitated, "how is that girlfriend of yours?"

He looked around nervously. "Shall we go into a quieter place?"

They walked the campus and went into the empty auditorium. They climbed upstairs to the mezzanine. Roman looked around as they were walking to make sure no one was following them.

"She's safe," he said.

"Who? Helena?" Maria gasped.

"No," he shrugged his shoulders, "my girlfriend, Rebecca, I found her a hiding place."

"In your village?"

"No, are you crazy? It's too dangerous. In a far away, small farm, at my old uncle's."

Maria's chest began pounding. "Could you do the same for Helena?"

Roman wetted his lip. "You two are still… friends?"

"We'll always be friends, Roman! And you are her friend too. I need your help."

"They've taken many," Roman said and looked away, "I think it might be too late. They're liquidating the enclosure."

Maria's heart pounded fast. She knew what would happen to her if she was caught having this conversation. She knew what would happen to Roman as well. She appreciated him trusting her. "I think," she whispered, "I... *know*, that she's still there, Roman! I... *feel* her...!"

Roman smiled, "Well, let me see. I have one contact who gets in and out of the enclosure. I'll ask him to find out if she's still there."

"Oh Roman!" Maria shrieked, "It will mean the world to me!"

CHAPTER 16

Roman spotted Maria on campus. His eyes signaled her to follow him.

It had been three days since their last conversation. He now had some information.

Maria followed him through the university into the biology building, and into one of the labs. There was a door to a storage room. He had the keys. He opened the door and then quickly closed it behind them.

"The good news is," he whispered, looking at Maria's wide eyes, "that she's alive."

Maria shrieked, "I knew it." She crossed her chest, "Thank you God. Thank you!"

"The other good news is," he sighed, "that she is working outside the enclosure."

"Outside?! Does she…?"

Roman nodded. "Each morning she is taken out with some other women to a factory owned by the occupying army… Then they all go back in the evening. So… I guess that's good."

She looked at him. "Go on."

He sighed and looked away, "The bad news is," he continued nervously, "that they took her mother and one of her brothers."

"No."

Roman nodded.

Maria covered her face with her hands.

Roman sighed. "And… she's basically alone. She told my friend's friend, who met her yesterday, that we shouldn't bother about her."

"That we shouldn't *what?!*"

"Bother about her. That she'll soon join her family, wherever they are."

Maria clenched her fist. "We need to get her out!"

Roman sighed, "It's not that simple."

They heard a noise from behind the door. Steps. The steps came closer. Maria's heart stopped. Then the steps continued away.

She waited until the steps disappeared.

Roman whispered, "Even if we somehow manage to smuggle her out, we need to get her documents… It's very expensive, and quite risky…"

"I'm done with risky," Maria said. "I cannot live this way anymore!"

Roman was quiet.

Maria looked at him. "How much?"

"A forged ID costs twenty thousand."

"Twenty thousand?!" Maria's eyes grew wide, "How can *anyone* come up with *twenty thousand?!*"

"You'd be surprised," Roman said.

Maria bit her lip. She shook her head.

Roman sighed, "I hate to tell you that, but even if we get that ID, and fill up a fake name and number, one must still have several other documents, matching documents, which are even harder to get…"

Maria shook her head. She began crying.

Roman sighed, "They took Gisele too, and her whole family."

Maria's eyes widened, "Has the world gone *mad?!* This is hell on earth!"

"You're…" Roman whispered, "a believer, right?"

Maria nodded.

"So you'll have to pray. I pray all the time."

Maria nodded.

"Twenty thousand?" Maria's father exclaimed, "How on earth…?!"

Maria sat on her parent's bed, her eyes red. She whispered, trying not to wake up Eddie and Sasha in the living room. "And he said that even if we *get* that sum, it's not easy to find someone to sell one, and then there are other documents one must get as well…"

Mrs. Bozek pouted her lip, "The other day a damned soldier stopped me. He looked at my ID and then said, 'Insufficient verification!'"

Mrs. Bozek shook her head, "He examined everything I had – my birth certificate, city registration, high school diploma, everything, as if I was a criminal!"

Maria looked at them. "I have a thousand of my own money. I borrowed another five hundred from a friend, and another three hundred from another friend…"

Mr. Bozek's eyes grew larger, "I don't want you going around asking for money. It will get people talking."

Maria's chin quivered, "I don't care, Papa! They took Helena's whole family! And Gisele is gone too…"

She began crying.

Mr. Bozek said, "I can only come up with five hundred myself," he opened the closet and moved a box aside, opening a small hidden place in the wall. "That's all I have, Marinka. We've exhausted everything…"

Mrs. Bozek fidgeted with her fingers. "Not everything."

She took off her wedding ring. "This used to be worth some fifteen thousand, maybe more…—"

"Mama! Are you sure…—"

126

Mrs. Bozek pursed her lip in determination, and handed Maria the ring. "Now go and fetch the poor girl, do whatever you need to do."

Maria nodded. Mr. Bozek crossed himself. They all did.

CHAPTER 17

"Dearest H.

I miss you terribly. It seems like I am able to procure you an empty ID. Please do your utmost efforts to get me a suitable photo of yours. I will anticipate for it tomorrow, or at the latest the day after. Please don't lose hope. Yours, always,

M."

"Dearest M.,

I do appreciate your efforts. As not to offend you, I've attached the photo you've asked for. But I beg you not to do anything foolish. They've hung a girl who tried to get her fiancé out. It's too dangerous. I'm fine here. I hope to soon join my family.

Yours, H."

"Dearest H.

Please give anything of value to the boy carrying this letter. Leave nothing in the enclosure of value. In one of the coming days, when the ID is prepared and stamped with your photo, I will come to take you, possibly in one of the mornings on your way to work. Please be prepared.

Hang on.

M."

CHAPTER 18

Maria climbed the stairs of a building not too far away from the entrance to the enclosure. The small windows of the stairway were dirty. She climbed to the third floor and looked down from the small window.

From there she could see the entrance to the enclosure. Four soldiers with rifles stood there, talking.

She memorized the names mounted on the doors of the second floor and the first floor. This was in case someone living in the building would ask her what she was doing there, and then she could say she came to visit someone…

She shook her head. It was a weak story. But it was the best she could come up with.

Outside the sun was just breaking over the horizon. Maria looked at her clock, a quarter past six.

She waited.

Thirty minutes later she finally saw something. On

the horizon, in the main street of the enclosure, a group of men appeared. They marched toward the gate of the enclosure. They wore their armbands visible even from this distance.

They looked horribly thin.

She still could not see their faces, but it seemed like all of them were men.

Those damned armbands, she thought. They were as bright as anything.

The soldiers opened the gate, and then led the group of men out. Then the gate closed behind them. Maria gasped at the number of soldiers escorting the group. Seven soldiers, no, eight soldiers with rifles.

Maria's heart beat fast. It was going to be more difficult than she had thought.

As the group passed by the building she was watching from, she looked at their faces. Helena was not there.

Few minutes of silence continued. Maria saw a few people walking in the street outside the enclosure's gate. The city was slowly waking up.

Her legs hurt from standing so long, on her tip-toes, looking out the window. Then - she saw them. A group of women marching on the horizon, down the main street of the enclosure. She bit her lip.

Her heart pounded. The soldiers opened the gate. The group of women was led by only one soldier. As they came out, though, Maria noticed another soldier walking behind them. She looked carefully at every face. All the women looked so gaunt. She hadn't seen Helena in over a year and a half. She worried that she would not recognize her best friend.

Finally, she realized that Helena was not in the group Tears came to her eyes as she thought that perhaps she had come too late - perhaps they had already taken Helena.

Her heart pounded. No. Please don't, God. Please, God, please. Please.

Just then, she saw another group of women led by a soldier, emerging in the distance, walking down the street inside the enclosure. She looked at her pocket watch. It was now three minutes before seven.

Then she saw her.

She gasped.

Was it indeed her?

The soldiers opened the gate, and the one at the head of the group led the row marching toward the building. Maria nodded to herself. That's Helena!

She ran down the stairs.

She exited the building. She saw the group of women walking on the sidewalk across the street. She walked quickly, trying not to attract attention to herself. Roman had told her the ID should be ready yesterday. Her heart pounded. She needed to be prepared.

She walked on the other side of the street. The women looked so feeble, their armbands so bright. They were walking tightly together, almost as if they were holding each other up.

The soldier at the back of the group looked at her. She looked away. Damn! She needed to be more careful.

She hoped her face didn't reveal her intentions. She wanted so badly to get a closer glimpse of Helena. But she knew it was not wise. The soldier leading the front turned right to the large street with the tram in its center.

Maria waited for the soldier at the back of the group to turn as well, and then she walked behind them, keeping a great distance.

More people filled the streets, hurrying to work. She kept her eyes on the group as they walked the pavement. Then she gasped. The group disappeared into one of the buildings.

She cursed to herself.

This route was impossible. It was too short.

She walked to that building. The occupying army's banner stretched over it. A soldier stood at the front. She continued walking.

She crossed the street and made her way back. This route was impossible. They only walked out of the enclosure, down the street, and then turning right at the central street, straight toward their factory.

Her face revealed her frustration. With a soldier at the front and a soldier at the back, this was just… impossible. How could she take Helena away?

She traced her steps back. She turned left at the corner back to the street leading to the enclosure.

She then made her way from her "lookout"

building down the street, experiencing the walk as if she was one of them. She looked at the shops on the way, trying not to attract attention to herself from passersby.

That was when she then saw a narrow passage between two buildings.

She walked down the passage, away from the street. Could they escape from here?

She was disappointed to see it was a dead end, leading to the back of one of the buildings. It was too dangerous. Even if she ran with Helena here, they'll still have to go back out to the street.

She was exasperated.

She was upset with Roman. "What do you mean it 'isn't ready'?!"

Roman looked offended, "I told you, Maria, that I'll do whatever I can, but the person handling the ID has many…"

"I don't care!" Maria exclaimed.

"Shhh" Roman whispered. The lab in the biology building was deserted, but you still never knew who was lurking nearby.

The air in the small storage room was stuffy.

"You said," Maria whispered, "that it would take a day or two, not a week!"

"I'm going to him every day, and…"

"I want to go and see this man! I gave my mother's wedding ring for it, and I'm not going to…—"

"Maria," he whispered, "this is a matter for grown ups, not of…—"

"I'm twenty three and so are you, Roman," she whispered, her eyes shining, "and you'll be taking me to see him today!"

Roman sighed, "I promised him I'd keep his work a secret…"

"Roman! It's Helena! It's Helena I'm talking about…" Maria bit her lip, trying not to cry, "It's our *Helena!* 'Stars circle round thy head, and at thy feet surges the sea, upon whose hurrying waves…'" her eyes watered, she put her chin out, "It's our Helena!"

Roman nodded.

Maria grabbed his coat, "It's our Helena, Roman! They could be butchering her right now, and you and I will have to live with the blood on our hands…!"

Roman's eyes watered. "I'll take you to him this afternoon."

Maria shook her head, "You'll take me to him now."

The man opened the door slightly, with the door chain still on. "Who are you?!"

Roman looked at him, surprised, "I'm… I was here yesterday and the day before…"

"I don't know you!" the man said and looked at Maria, "The people I know don't bring spies with them!"

Maria looked at the man behind the door with her fiery eyes. "I'm not a spy," she muttered, "and unless you want me to become one, you'll open the door right now."

The door slammed in their faces.

Roman shook his head. "Maria...!"

Maria raised her chin up.

Suddenly they heard the door's chain jingled. Roman's eyes grew bigger. The door opened slightly. The man motioned to them to come in, quickly. They walked in.

The man looked down the stairway and closed the door, locking it with three locks. "No one followed you here?"

Roman shook his head, "No, I looked."

The man sighed, "Now why do you bring me this trouble!"

Roman was about to say something, but Maria interrupted. "Sir, I'm the one who gathered the remaining money of my family, including my mother's...—"

"Spare me your words, girl, I hear these stories all the time..."

Maria was taken aback, "You'll hear me until I'm done!"

The man's eyes grew bigger, as did Roman's. Maria

muttered through her teeth, "Now you're either going to get me that ID right away, or I will open that window there and scream to the whole street what you are doing here."

The man shook his head. He sighed, "I have IDs from three weeks ago waiting, I'm only one man…"

"I'll help you if you need," Maria said, "But we're not leaving this place until I have that ID!"

He looked at her, puzzled.

She looked at him, her eyes fiery. "My best friend's life is on the line. Now, shall we get to it, or do you need more drama?"

The man suddenly smiled. He looked baffled. He went to his bookcase, moved some books around, and pulled the whole bookcase away from the wall. It revealed a small desk with a pile of IDs on it. Maria felt her heart beat as she saw the IDs.

The man shuffled through the pile. "Now, what was her name again…?"

"Helena," Maria said and came closer, "Helena Goldstein."

He looked through the photos. "Is that her?"

Maria looked over his shoulder. It was her Helena. "Yes!"

He took a breath and placed the photo next to him. He took an empty ID and a black pen. "Shall I just invent a name," the man said, "or do you…"

"Invent?!" Maria cried, "don't you have some list of… names…?"

He shrugged his shoulders, "I invent the names. Then people forge documents accordingly elsewhere..."

Maria bit her lip. She looked at Roman, who looked rather helpless, and asked him, "What name did you give your girlfriend?"

"I didn't. Rebecca is in hiding. If she were to be found then..."

"And can Helena also...?"

Roman shook his head, "My uncle already said he's too afraid of having just one...—"

"I see." Maria breathed heavily.

The man looked at her, "I'm sorry but I don't have the whole day."

"Give her my name. Maria Bozek."

The man looked at her, raised his eyebrows, and turned around to look at Roman.

Roman looked at her, "Maria, that's... too dangerous... If they find out...—"

"What else do you offer!" Maria shrieked, "You two are constantly telling me what *not* to do, but you offer no help!"

"But... Maria..." Roman mumbled, "your family. They can kill them all..."

The man looked at her, "The punishment for giving someone your ID is death..."

Maria reached for her purse. "This way I could give her my birth certificate, and high school diploma," she sighed, "and the baptismal certificate…" she took her ID out and put it on the man's desk. "Copy it."

The man shrugged his shoulders, "They are very clever… They match the registry…"

Maria spoke quietly. "Please copy it."

The man looked at Roman again and shook his head, "I'm afraid you don't know what you're…"

Maria muttered at him, "Copy it now I say!"

CHAPTER 19

The sun was just rising. Only a few shops had opened. Maria was waiting, hiding in the narrow passage between the two buildings. Roman was near the tram station down the street. He had warned her. "We need a better plan," he said, "possibly someone from within the enclosure could somehow smuggle her out at night..."

But Maria would have none of it. These were all ideas, empty ideas, without a concrete way of implementation. Options for the future. Vague ideas. She felt her time running out.

Roman insisted, "But the risk, you can't just grab her like that on the street!"

"That's exactly what I'll do."

"But they'll shoot you. You'll kill yourself and her!"

"Roman," Maria shook her head, "where is Gisele? Where are Helena's brothers? Her parents? Where are they all?"

"They were taken…"

"Taken where, Roman?"

Roman was silent.

"Wake up, Roman! We've all been blinded! We cannot continue waiting! Every minute we waste might be the Helena's last…!"

"But, Maria…"

"All I need is for you to speak to your uncle. I can't take her home. It's too visible, too dangerous, everyone knows her. We'll get Helena to your uncle's farm. Then I'll figure it out. Just for a day."

Roman sighed. He wanted so badly to say 'no', but he knew he couldn't. He knew he could never forgive himself if he refused to cooperate, and if Helena would then… "But," he said, "I'm taking no part in your crazy abduction! It's doomed to fail, Maria! I can convince my uncle to hide her in his barn for one night, maybe. But I'm not going to endanger her and you by cooperating…—"

"That's fine," Maria said, "I've done my homework."

Now her heart pounded. She was doubting her plan. Had she, indeed, done her homework?

She put her hands on two fur scarfs. She thought it would help Helena look more dignified, and disguise that poor dress she had seen her with two days earlier.

She took a deep breath in. The fur will do *something*, she thought. She needed to get Helena quickly to the tram for a short ride to the train station, where they'd get her out of the city and to the farm. Then they'd see what to do next.

She saw a few people passing in the street. It was six thirty in the morning. She pretended to look at the names on the mail boxes, fearing one of the neighbors might come out of their home.

Yes, she thought, the scarf would do something. One of the earliest stipulations the occupying army was for all 'enemies' not to wear fur. The fur scarf could make Helena, now, look less like she's one of *them*.

But Maria knew she'd also have to get rid of the horrific armband instantly.

She suddenly heard the steps, marching down the street. She bit her lip. It was the men. She knew. She saw the first soldier marching down the pavement, so close to her. She saw the men with their armbands, bent over in weakness, walking, surrounded by other soldiers with their rifles.

She pressed her back against the wall, not wanting them to see her.

She closed her eyes and nodded to herself. This was the best plan. The best plan. Here, between these buildings, right near the corner. The lead soldier would be in the front, he wouldn't see. And the soldier at the back of the row would still be around the corner, he wouldn't see either, right?

She breathed heavily. God, she prayed, make the other women in the line say nothing. God, good God, make it work. Make it work.

She kept praying in her heart, now moving away

143

from the wall as to not seem odd. She stared at the mailboxes. She then heard it. Another group. The steps were distinct. She looked out to the street. She saw some people passing by, probably on the way to work. Then she saw the soldier coming. She gasped and pressed her body against the wall. She saw the women with the armbands walking. She looked carefully, walking closer, just in case Helena might somehow gotten into this group. She looked at their faces intently. Being in such close proximity to them, Maria suddenly thought how instead of grabbing Helena, she should reach and hug her, then carry her into the passage. In case one of the soldiers noticed, she could then explain she just… passed by… and suddenly saw her old friend. Hugging a person is not a crime, right?

Her heart beat heavily. What a lame story. They'd probably shoot her. She had already heard similar stories. The soldiers were merciless.

The women's row ended, followed by a soldier with his rifle. Soon, Maria thought. She prayed again.

She thought she heard the steps of the other group coming down the street. She tried listening. No. Not yet.

Any moment now.

Then she heard the steps. The soldier appeared on the pavement, walking quickly. Then the first woman. Not Helena. Then the next, not Helena either. That's not Helena. That's not Helena. That's not Helena…

Her heart nearly burst out her chest.

That's not Helena. That's not Helena. That's

Helena. "Helena!" she exclaimed jumping over the thin woman. Helena's eyes grew bigger, anticipating a bullet shooting at her at any moment. Maria grabbed her and ran with her into the narrow passage, then she pressed herself against the wall. Helena did the same, looking at her, terrified.

They heard the footsteps continuing. Maria's lip tightened, whitening. Footsteps. More footsteps. They looked at each other.

Then the footsteps ceased.

"Quick," Maria whispered, placing her second fur scarf on Helena's neck. She grabbed Helena's armband and tore it off in one strong movement. The dress tore around the arm. She looked at the armband in her hand. Where should she put it? Taking it would be detrimental, leaving it behind would be stupid as well. She saw the mailboxes and shoved it into one of them. Helena looked at her, petrified. Maria breathed heavily, "You're name is Maria Bozek. Now," she tried to stabilize her breath. She put her purse on Helena's shoulder. "Now we'll go, calmly," she wetted her lip, "Roman is waiting for us at the tram station. Let's go. Calmly, we're just *regular people*," she adjusted the fur scarf on Helena's neck.

She put Helena's arm in her arm. They walked a few steps. Suddenly Helena stopped. "But…" she murmured, "If… if *I'm* Maria, then… if we get asked… then who are *you*…?"

Maria forced a smile, "Leave that to me." She pulled Helena and they began walking. They exited the narrow passage and took a sharp left, away from the group that passed moments before. They walked quickly. Maria focused on the tram station in the distance. She bit her lip and then forced herself to smile. She straightened her back, pulled her shoulders back, and nudged Helena to do the same. People passed near them. Maria told herself, we're just regular people. Just friends, going to work.

Maria tried to resist her instinct to run. It would look odd if they ran. She glanced at Helena, who looked pale as a ghost. Maria muttered from between her teeth, "Smile!"

Helena forced a smile. They walked quickly. The tram station was closer. Maria could see Roman standing there. They walked faster. Roman looked wide-eyed at Helena. Maria slowed their steps, now standing along the other few people waiting for the tram. She didn't want to look back at where they came from. Where is the tram? Each second felt like a long minute. She looked back. In the distance, she thought she saw the group of women, down the street, entering the factory. She saw the large banner of the occupying army. She looked in the horizon thinking, "*Where is the tram?!*"

Then she saw it. The tram made its way slowly through the street. Good. But then her heart stopped beating as she watched a soldier come out of the factory, running down the street, holding his rifle, and then another soldier following him, running too. She looked away. Helena did the same. The tram made its way toward the station, slowing down. The tram's doors opened. Maria nearly pushed Helena through the tram's door, quickly paying the driver for the two of them. Through the glass she saw the soldiers running toward them. She couldn't move.

She forced herself to sit down, Helena joining her. She looked in the other direction, willing the tram to begin moving. She told herself, "We're just regular people... just regular people. God, please!"

Never in her life did she invoke God's name as intensely and purposefully as she did in that moment. The other people climbed into the tram, Roman among them. The driver closed the doors. Roman, standing not too far from Maria and Helena, looked in the direction where Maria refused to look. His eyes widened as he saw the soldiers approaching the intersection. But then, the soldiers turned toward the street leading to the enclosure, away from the tram. The tram began moving, gaining speed. Roman sighed a sigh of relief and nodded at Maria. She bit her lip. A tear fell down her cheek.

CHAPTER 20

The three of them got off the tram near the train station. None of them dared saying a word while they were on the tram. Now Roman said only, "Follow me."

Maria and Helena followed, arm in arm.

They entered the train station, heading to the platform. Roman suddenly turned around, heading in the other direction. Maria's eyes widened as she saw two soldiers checking people's IDs. She turned around too, and Helena, startled, nearly tripped.

They walked quickly in the other direction. Roman knew the train station well. They walked down some stairs, and then back up, approaching the platform from the other entrance.

But then, just as they came up the stairs, they saw a soldier examining people's IDs.

Maria saw Roman hesitating, and whispered to him, "Keep going." She knew turning around only a few steps from the soldier would not look good.

"Documents!" the soldier barked.

They stood before him, on the platform at the top of the stairs. Roman quickly handed the soldier his ID, and Helena, her hands trembling, found the ID in the purse Maria had given her. Maria shook her head firmly, "I don't have mine, it was stolen yesterday!"

"Stolen?!" the soldier exclaimed.

"I went to the police station and filed a report, and this morning I went to the Interior Office, but they weren't open yet!"

He looked at her, surveying her face. Her chin was raised, and she looked at him straight in the eyes. "Maybe," she muttered, "if soldiers like you were doing their jobs *properly*, people's things wouldn't be stolen like this!"

Roman's eyes widened. Helena looked down at the floor. This seemed foolish.

The soldier looked at Maria, clenching his jaw. She quickly added, "I'm certain that under *your* shift such things don't happen! But your friends *do* need to be reprimanded for allowing such things…"

"Enough!" he exclaimed. He looked at Roman's ID. "Date of birth!"

Roman muttered, "September 12th, 1919."

The soldier raised the ID to his eye level, looked at Roman and at the photo in the ID. He pouted his lip, "Insufficient verifications!"

"I also have," Roman mumbled, "these." He handed some documents to the soldier.

The train heading out of the city approached the platform.

The soldier looked through the documents and sighed. He nodded, and handed Roman the ID and the documents. He then looked at Helena's ID.

Maria stopped her breath. "If you please, Sir, we don't want to miss the train!"

"One more word," the soldier said and stared at Maria, "and I'll throw you straight to jail. There's a death penalty for losing government documents!"

Maria stared at him, not taking her gaze off.

"Date of birth!" the soldier barked at Helena.

She smiled, "January 22nd, 1920."

He looked at the ID, raised it, looked at the photo, then at her, then back at the photo. "Insufficient verification." He said and sighed.

Helena smiled, "Of course, forgive me." She reached for her purse. She looked at the documents, hesitating. Would there be a photo of Maria there? Did Maria actually make… She fidgeted through the documents, then handing him all she had. He unfolded the papers. He looked at the name of the birth certificate, the baptism certificate, and the school's diploma. He nodded and handed Helena the ID and the documents, "That's fine, Miss Bozek".

Helena smiled, "Thank you," she took her purse and placed the documents and the ID inside.

Maria suddenly saw the soldier's eyes widening. He looked at Helena. Maria's heart stopped beating. What did he see?

He exclaimed, "Miss Bozek!"

Maria looked down, and then caught herself. He was speaking to Helena.

The soldier barked, pointing at Helena's arm, "Why is your dress torn here?!"

"Where?" Helena asked, "Oh, this? It's just," she laughed, "that I haven't had the time yet to stitch…—"

The soldier's ground his teeth and reached for the whistle around his neck. Roman thought of launching and running away. Maria looked, wide-eyed, at Helena.

But Helena burst into loud laughter, and then said in a rather flirtatious tone, "I hope I'm not too provocatively dressed for you, Mr. soldier, sir…?"

Roman watched the train's doors close and saw it leaving the station. They were doomed.

The soldier didn't fall into Helena's trap. "That's!" he exclaimed and pointed at her arm, "That's where the armband is worn on the…—"

Helena gasped and crossed herself, "Jesus, Mary and Joseph! Never ever!" she cried, "Don't compare me to *them*, sir!"

He looked at her face, then at the torn dress, then at her face again.

"Hans!"

They all looked over their shoulders at the other platform. An officer stood there, waving at the soldier in front of them. In front of the officer there were two old people and a child. The officer looked at the soldier, "Hans! I need you here!"

The soldier, whose name must have been Hans, now lowered the whistle, "I'll be there!" he shouted.

He looked at Helena, shaking his head. He then looked at Maria and pointed his finger at her, "You! If I see you again without documents, I'll *shoot* you there and then!"

Maria nodded and smiled a sour smile.

The soldier then hurried down the stairs heading to the other platform.

Roman looked at Helena and then at Maria, speechless. Maria began walking, "Let's go."

They went and sat at the end of the platform, waiting for the train. They saw how the officer, on the other platform, now assisted by the soldier who a moment earlier examined their IDs, took the older man with him. The soldier, Hans, grabbed the old woman's arms, and the child in his other hand. The child didn't want to go, and began screaming and crying. He fell on the floor. The soldier dragged him by the hand, as the child tried holding on to people's legs. People stepped away. None of the people in that platform said or did anything.

The screaming child disappeared into the train's offices.

Maria looked at the scene, and saw how Helena gazed at the floor, not looking.

CHAPTER 21

"I cannot hide another one!" the old uncle muttered.

"Uncle, it's only for one night."

"That's what you said of Rebecca, 'only for a little while', and now you're putting me an impossible situation Roman!"

Maria looked at Helena, holding her hand, sitting in the living room. Roman and the uncle were whispering to each other in the kitchen.

Roman insisted, "One night, uncle! I promise."

The uncle whispered, "The neighbors in the market already noticed I'm buying too much food for one person…"

Roman said, "Uncle, please! Just for one night!"

The uncle sighed. There was a long silence. "You are tightening the rope around my neck, you childish boy. Do you know what the soldiers can do?"

"Thank you so much, Uncle…"

Roman left the kitchen. "Let's go," he said, and

opened the back door leading to the barn.

They followed him. The uncle walked out of the kitchen, shaking his head disapprovingly.

Roman led them to the barn. They looked at the piles of hay. Roman whispered, "Sweetie? Rebecca? It's me…!"

They saw a pile of hay moving, then another, and a ragged looking young woman came out. Maria was horrified. She looked so different than the pretty girl she remembered.

Roman and his girlfriend embraced. She exclaimed, "I missed you!" she then noticed Maria and Helena. "Who are they?"

"Friends from school," Roman said, "My friends Maria and…—"

Maria quickly interrupted, "and *Maria*. Pleased to meet you! I believe I've seen you before."

The girlfriend sighed. "Before the war…?"

Maria nodded.

Roman took Rebecca by the hand and said, "Let's give them some privacy."

They went behind one of the large piles of hay.

Helena looked around the small barn. She looked hopeless.

Maria looked at her and whispered, "I'll get you out of here. Don't worry."

Helena nodded. She said nothing, leaned on one of the hay piles, and slouched on the ground.

Maria looked at her, worried. There was something in Helena's gaze... her eyes looked... hollow.

"Eddie and Sashinka," Maria said cheerfully, "have been asking about you." She sat down on the ground, leaning against the stack of hay.

Helena said slowly, as if waking up from a dream, "Did they...?"

Maria nodded. To herself she thought, 'Where is my Helena? This person isn't my Helena!'" She shook her head. "Eddie is in the polytechnic high school, doing well, and Sashinka is going next year to *our* school!"

Helena nodded.

Maria tried smiling, "She's almost our age when we first met..."

Helena nodded her head slowly. "So long ago..."

Maria couldn't stop her tears from coming. What had happened to Helena? She shook her head. No, she needs to be the strong one. She wouldn't cry.

Roman and Rebecca were kissing in the corner of the barn. They could hear them.

Helena stared into the air, blurry eyed.

Maria looked at her, "Helena..."

Helena did not respond.

Maria shook her, "Helena! Do you hear me?!"

Helena moved her shoulder, slowly, like a child not wanting to do something. She stared into the air. Then she said slowly, "The other women... they said nothing…"

"The other women?"

"In the line… when… you took me…"

"Yes," Maria said quickly, "that was good, right?"

Helena nodded slowly. "Whenever someone… disappeared… we were happy for her …"

Maria nodded. "Of course, Helena!"

"I don't know… what happened to Reuben…"

Maria hesitated. She didn't want to ask.

"My name… my name was on the list," she said, "Reuben, he paid to someone to switch my name with his. Then they took him. And my Mother... But Solomon and Hannah hid… They are still hiding in the enclosure…" She looked at Maria in the eyes, "I should try… and help them…"

Maria folded her hands together nervously, "You should help yourself first, Helena…"

Maria felt awful saying that.

Helena nodded, "Solomon is smart… he'll find a way… But Reuben… I wonder where he is now…"

Maria said, "Shhh…" and put her arm around Helena, pulling her to her lap, "Here, rest on me, Helena…"

Helena did not resist. She laid there in Maria's arms.

Maria noticed how thin Helena was. She bit her lip. Tears began flowing down her eyes.

Helena didn't cry. She stared into the air. "I wonder... where they are... Have you ever found out where they sent my Father?"

Maria hesitated, "No dear... I haven't..."

CHAPTER 22

Maria entered the house.

Her mother jumped first, then her father, then Eddie and Sasha. "Where were you?"

Maria tried smiling, "I have good news."

She locked the door behind her, and hugged her mother. She whispered, "Let's go to the kitchen."

Her mother nodded.

In the small kitchen, they had all finished their dinner. They looked at her eagerly.

Maria smiled, "She's safe."

Sasha asked, "Who? Helena?"

"Shhh…" everyone hushed her.

Mrs. Bozek clasped her hands together, "Now sit and tell us everything."

Maria took her coat off and sat near the table. Her mother served her hot potatoes. "No. So speak!"

"Roman," Maria whispered, "has an uncle, and

he'll be hiding her for the night."

Mr. Bozek leaned forward, "And then?"

Maria shook her head, "I don't know."

Mrs. Bozek tut-tutted, "She's not going to hide, right? The ID you got should..."

"No, I don't want her to hide. I think the enclosure had already done some... damage... She's not well..."

Mr. Bozek stared at her, "What do you mean?"

Maria shrugged her shoulders. "She's..." her lip pouted, "She's..."

Maria began crying. Eddie put his hand on her.

"She's..." Maria shook her head, looking at them all, "She's.... so *fragile*..."

Mrs. Bozek exclaimed, "She needs to eat!"

"No," Maria said, "it's not that... not *only* that... she's... she seems..." she put her hands on her face, "broken..."

Her father shook his head. "Those bastards..."

Sasha asked, "What will you do, Maria?"

"I don't know!" Maria exclaimed, sobbing.

No one dared saying anything. Mrs. Bozek finally said, "Well, she cannot stay there in hiding, nor can she come to the city..."

Eddie mumbled, "People will recognize her..."

Silence ensued. Maria wiped her tears.

Mrs. Bozek looked helpless. "Eat your food,

Maria!"

Maria nodded, but didn't touch it. "She needs to go to a large city…"

Her father interrupted. "We need to get her to the capital."

"I thought so too," Maria said, "but… I can't go with her."

"Why not?" her mother asked.

Maria hesitated. She didn't tell them.

They all looked at her. She took a deep breath. "I… I gave her… my name…"

"You did *what?*" Mrs. Bozek cried.

"She needed," Maria said, "not only the ID, but also the other documents, you know, Mama. So, I gave her mine. I'll get new ones."

Mr. Bozek shook his head, "That's dangerous, Maria."

Maria nodded, tears flowing again, "Papa, what should I have done? You saw how difficult it was to get the ID itself, how could I get forged documents, and how long would it have taken me…?"

Mrs. Bozek looked at her husband.

He sighed. "You did well."

Maria looked at him with her big eyes, "Yes, Papa?"

He nodded. He got up and walked the small kitchen back and forth. "Surely you cannot go with her. No two Maria Bozeks can be…"

Maria nodded, "And with the same date of birth, and everything."

Mrs. Bozek shook her head. "This is too dangerous. Our family is now on the line…"

Mr. Bozek said, "We need to somehow get her to the capital. Someone we trust will need to go with her. Then we need to get her a job of some kind…"

Mrs. Bozek sighed and looked at her husband, "You have your friend there, the old Mr. Winton…"

Maria looked at him, "Could you, Papa, write to him?"

Mr. Bozek sighed. "I can see what I can do…"

Maria looked hopeful. "Now I just need to find someone to take the couple of days off and go with her…"

Mr. Bozek said, "I wished I could, but I cannot leave work, the manager said…—"

"I can do it," Eddie said.

Maria's eyes widened. "Really? Eddie?"

Eddie nodded. Maria looked at her father, "Papa, is that okay?"

Mr. Bozek sighed and looked at Eddie.

"I'll be fine," Eddie said, "I'll say we're brother and sister, if the soldiers…"

"Not *if*," Mr. Bozek exclaimed, "*when*! You'll be questioned several times, 'What do you do going to the capital', 'What business you have there…'"

Mrs. Bozek shrieked, "Can they find out that ID is

fake?"

Maria shrugged her shoulders, "I hope not…"

Mrs. Bozek crossed her chest, "Jesus, Mar,y and Joseph!"

Silence followed.

Maria looked at Eddie. Then she looked at her mother, who shook her head. Her eyes were moist. Then Maria looked at her father, and at Sasha. She sighed, "It's what we need to do. She has no more…" she bit her lip, "She has no more family but us…"

Her father nodded. "Eddie will go with her."

Maria fell on her young brother's shoulder, "Eddinka, you'll watch her, right? And yourself, right?"

Eddie nodded.

Mr. Bozek sighed, "I'll give you a letter to Mr. Winton. Is that farm she's in safe? Where does she hide there?"

"In the barn," Maria murmured.

Mr. Bozek shook his head and looked at Eddie, "You'll need to go tomorrow."

Mrs. Bozek stood up, "I'll… prepare food for you! You make sure Helena eats, okay Eddinka?"

Eddie nodded. He looked at his big sister. "She'll be safe with me."

CHAPTER 23

Standing on the crowded platform, Maria waved goodbye to Eddie and Helena.

Helena smiled through the window. She had her valise with her. And a box with potatoes, spinach, and even some meat, which Mrs. Bozek had prepared throughout the night. Eddie nodded at Maria, assuring her with his eyes that all will be okay.

Maria tried letting go. Oh, how much she would have liked to be there on the train to hold Helena's hand. But Helena did seem better this morning. A bit.

She folded her hands together, looking at poor Helena. Could the soldiers somehow find out that Helena's ID was fake? That the stamp, in fact, was stamped in a dodgy apartment by an unknown man for an unbelievable sum? Would Helena be able to deal with soldiers questioning her on the way?

Maria looked at Eddie. Was she doing the right thing, sending him off this way? He was still a kid. Yes, he was seventeen, but he was still so young.

As the train began moving, she waved goodbye to them. They waved back, until they disappeared. The other people on the platform slowly walked away. But Maria stayed there, lingering, as if keeping her gaze on the disappearing train could somehow protect two of the most important people in her entire world.

CHAPTER 24

"Dear Maria,

Please thank Eddie in my name. He's been so kind, and so mature! Staying with me for whole three days, helping me with all of the arrangements... renting a room... I'm so proud of him!

Also, please thank your dear mother, for the food which reminded me of the festive times we had together. Please also thank your dear Father for writing to Mr. Winton. He was able to procure me a job at the train station, beginning tomorrow. I have no words to express my gratitude.

I feel better now. I realize I wasn't really in my right mind when we met. I am much better now. I look forward to the next time I'll see you.

Again, please thank Eddie and give him a big hug. He showed courage several times. I will tell you all when we meet again, whenever that will be. Hopefully sooner than we think.

Yours,

Maria."

CHAPTER 25

"Dear Maria,

I was so happy to see Eddie come back, and bringing such good news from you!

I cannot tell you how happy I was reading your letter, I read it again and again. You sound much more vital and strong. I do hope you are feeling better and better each day. I do hope that soon everything will pass, and we can be reunited in our beloved city.

I keep praying for good news about your whole family. Miracles do happen, as long as we believe in them.

Please send Mr. Winton my love, as I remember him well from his visits in my childhood.

Do write to me more, I've missed you terribly.

Yours,

Maria."

CHAPTER 26

"Dear Maria,

It's been a year now, and the work at the train station has been satisfactory indeed. I am now in charge of the announcements. It's as close as you've imagined of me getting "famous". I am certainly famous among the passengers, and I can assure you that all the passengers listen to my words attentively. Never before have I had such large audiences!

I do miss our beloved city, though. Please walk to the city hall's fountain for me once in awhile. I remember fondly feeding the doves and pigeons there.

I went to a ballet performance a week ago. Since then I cannot stop singing.

Do tell me about your progress on your seminary about erythromycin (I hope I spelled it correctly). It sounds so exciting, what you wrote about antibiotics. Terrific!

I am more settled now here, and I enjoy the city life. There is much more I want to write to you, but it will have to wait until we meet again. Do send my love to the family. How is Sashinka doing? She must be enjoying school. Did you take her to our hiding place on the roof?

I miss you terribly. Do write to me quickly, as I anticipate your letters all the time.

Yours always,

Maria."

CHAPTER 27

"Dear Maria,

Your letter brought so much joy to my heart. I cannot believe I haven't seen you for so long… When this season passes, seeing you will be the first thing I'll look forward to!

I was sorry to hear of Mr. Winton's passing. But I am happy to hear that you are well, and that your job is secure.

We are all well. Sasha is a sweetheart. She actually reminds me a lot of you. She now prefers 'Sasha' over 'Sashinka', and gives me a hard time whenever I misaddress her. She loves novels, and reads a lot. I wish you were present in her life at this crucial age, as you were in mine.

I promised her that when things change, you and I will take her to the sea.

Eddie is in his last year, doing well in school. He works a lot in the afternoons as a delivery boy. He thinks of studying engineering in university. I'm so happy for him. He has become little man, could you believe it? He reminds me a lot of papa.

I hope my pharmaceutical study paper won't bore you – but I thought you might enjoy the research I've done. You should go back to university when this season ends... Studying is so pleasurable...

The mail has been faulty, and I saw that your previous letter arrived two weeks later. Such things did not happen before this season. I do hope things will change soon. I pray for it each day.

My mother keeps praying and sending her love, as my father and Eddie and Sasha do too. I look forward to hearing from you as soon as possible.

Yours, Maria."

"Dear Maria,

Have you received my last two letters? I have yet to hear from you. Please respond to me, at least signaling that you are well. I get anxious not hearing from you!

Papa and Mama, Eddie and Sasha send their love. Do write to me promptly!

Yours,

Maria."

"Dear Maria,

It's been two months since I heard from you last. I wrote to Sofia, and she said she does not know where you are, and that you've been missing from the train station for some time now.

Please, I beg you! If you receive this letter, do write to me promptly. I am terribly agonized with uncertainty.

Maria."

CHAPTER 28

Travelling to the capital on an overnight train, alone, Maria Bozek could not close an eye. Neither could she read or eat. She was too distraught.

When the train arrived at the capital in the morning, Maria immediately got off the train and took a taxi to the western train station.

Arriving at the train station, she reached for her pocket. There she had a photo of Helena. But she was afraid to approach anyone or to show it. She had a bad feeling.

She saw a woman behind the window at the ticket counter. After hesitating for some time, she decided to ask her. She stood in the line until her turn came.

"Where to?" the woman in the window asked.

"Could I," Maria whispered, "have a word with you?"

The woman raised her eyebrows, "Do I know you?"

"No, but you may know my friend, Maria Bozek.

She used to work here."

The woman's eyes grew larger. "I don't know her, and you better not know her either!"

Maria sensed an alarm in the woman's voice.

There were people behind her in line. The woman behind the window exclaimed, nearly yelling, "Next please!"

Maria moved over. Now her bad feeling became a knot in her stomach.

She walked outside the station. She was determined to find out.

She decided to wait until that woman finished work.

Maria waited until the evening. She kept her eyes on the door near the ticket booth, afraid to go eat, even afraid to go and use the bathroom. She didn't want that lady to leave without seeing her.

When evening came the woman finally exited the booth. Maria followed her to the street.

The woman took the tram. Maria took the tram as well.

Maria knew she could not speak about it in the tram. She decided to wait. The woman got off at the end of the line. Maria followed her.

She kept her distance as the woman walked the small streets. Then the woman suddenly began running.

Maria ran after her. "Please," Maria called, "Please stop!"

The woman entered one of the buildings. Maria entered the building as well. The woman stopped on the staircase, panting, looking terrified at Maria, "What do you want from me?!"

"I'm looking for my friend," Maria whispered, "I told you in the morning…"

"You're…" the woman hesitated, "you're the woman who asked about…?"

Maria nodded.

They stood there, both panting, as the woman evaluated Maria. "Are you from the *underground*? I want nothing to do with the *resistance!*"

"Me neither!" Maria exclaimed, "I just need to know where my friend is!"

The woman looked at Maria for a long moment. Finally, she nodded. "Come with me."

Maria followed the woman as she climbed the stairs to the last floor. The woman looked down at the staircase, seeing no one had followed them. She opened the door, turned the light on, and signaled to Maria to enter, then locked the door behind them.

The woman then approached the window. She peaked around the curtains to see if there was anyone suspicious on the street. She looked at Maria, "Are you sure you came alone?"

Maria nodded.

"How do you know Maria?" the woman asked.

"She was," Maria said and then corrected herself, "she *is* my best friend."

The woman shook her head and whispered. "I think they took her."

Maria nearly fainted, "No!"

The woman walked away. Her eyes became teary. She looked back at Maria. "There was a small party," she said, "in the office. Maria used to read the announcements…"

Maria nodded.

"And we… sang some songs. One of the guys sang some…" she sighed, "some song against the occupying army."

Maria bit her lip, "And?"

"And we all sang along. The office was locked, so we felt free. And…" she sighed, "Maria joined along with her beautiful voice. But then we heard some commotion. It turned out the microphone was on."

"No!"

The woman nodded. "The whole station heard it. Maria understood it instantly, took her purse, and ran away. The guy who led the song also disappeared. They took him, and I think they took her."

Maria shook her head. "Did you *see* them take her?"

"No," the woman sighed, "but less than a minute later some soldiers came into the office inquiring who sang the song. When we said they were gone, they punished the whole management. I…" the woman's voice broke, "they took me to the police station. They interrogated me… for five hours…."

"I'm so sorry," Maria murmured.

The woman shook her head. "We would have heard something about Maria had she been alive. I think they took her."

Maria wanted to cry. "But you didn't *see* them take her?"

The woman shook her head.

Maria sighed, "That's all I need to know. Thank you for trusting me." Maria took a deep breath and headed toward the door.

"Wait," the woman said, "if you hear anything about her, good or bad, could you let me know? You now know where I live."

Maria nodded. She exited the apartment, descending the stairs, disappearing into the night.

CHAPTER 29

Maria wasn't herself anymore.

She had nightmares.

Eddie and Sasha pitied her. Her mother tried to encourage her. Her father told her to leave it to God.

But she was not willing to hear. "I let her down," she murmured. "I should have helped her get across the border, to run away. It was too dangerous for her... I should have known."

She barely ate.

She went to her old school, where Sasha was now studying, and climbed to the third floor. The window which once was so big, now seemed much smaller.

She climbed onto the roof. She sat there in the cold weather, crying. "Helena..." she whispered, "where are you?"

She searched her heart to see whether she could sense something. Was Helena alive? Was she dead? Was she safe?

Her heart told her nothing.

At university she couldn't concentrate. She told Roman what she had found out in her trip to the capital. He said he'd ask his contacts to see if he could find out anything.

But he came up with nothing.

Helena was gone. And Maria knew it was her own fault.

It was unfortunate, really, because the war seemed to be ending. After five years of unemployment, suffering, hunger, and terrible stories of murder and torture, it looked like an end was in sight.

The liberating allies were now attacking the occupying army fiercely.

The country was still occupied. But people understood the news reports. While the news was still filled with propaganda, people speculated that all the "realignments" and "repositioning" of the occupying army meant the approaching end of the war. The occupying army would be defeated soon, everybody hoped.

The occupying army was now madly trying to defend the borders. Trains were used to mobilize soldiers and ammunition toward the borders. Many civilian trains stopped working. The mail, too, was extremely faulty. The occupying army was screening most letters, fearing coded and hidden intelligence of the underground resistance movement cooperating with the liberating allies.

The atmosphere in the Bozek house now changed. Mr. Bozek was hopeful. He muttered at dinner, "Soon those bastards will be gone! Out of here for good!"

But Maria could not rejoice. She felt *guilty*. She felt *helpless*. It's been eight months now since Helena disappeared. Maria tried to remain hopeful, but she felt like she was simply deceiving herself.

She once thought to herself that somehow, in some way, this might be for the best. That Helena did *want* to join her parents and brothers. That this was somehow good.

But that thought depressed her even more.

Her mother begged her to eat, she had lost a lot of weight. She bought her a brand new dress, green with white lace. It was beautiful.

But Maria didn't want to wear it.

Each of the family members tried to speak to her separately. But nothing helped.

She continued to go to university, but the light was gone from her eyes. She often daydreamed. Her mind was filled with torturing thoughts. Helena shot. Helena raped. Helena thrown somewhere in some field calling her name, "Maria!" before she died.

CHAPTER 30

One evening there was a knock on the door.

Mr. Bozek answered and saw a tall man. "I'm looking for Miss Maria Bozek," he said.

"And *you* are?" Mr. Bozek barked. He didn't like the look of this man.

"I'm sorry, sir. I cannot say. I'm looking for Miss Maria Bozek."

Maria, hearing this from the kitchen, ran to the door. Her father blocked her from the door. "No!" he said, "I don't trust this man."

The tall man remained standing there. He looked at Maria coldly. "Are you Maria Bozek?"

"I am," she cried.

He nodded. "I have a letter. For you."

She cried, "From whom?"

"A woman, about your age." He looked at the street and lowered his voice, "Please spare me of saying her name out loud. I don't think it will be very wise," his eyes glared, "neither for her, nor for you."

Maria's eyes grew larger. Mr. Bozek shook his head, "It's a hoax. Where's the letter?"

The tall man clenched his jaw. "I've travelled a long distance to carry it for you. I deserve compensation. I expect two thousand for my efforts in cash."

Mr. Bozek reddened, "Two thousand for a letter!"

The man turned around.

"Wait!" Maria cried, "Papa, let me go!"

She escaped Mr. Bozek and ran to the street. Mr. Bozek remained at the door with Mrs. Bozek, Eddie and Sasha standing behind him.

Maria told the man, "Show me the letter."

The tall man looked down at her, and then at Mr. Bozek. He reached for his coat. "Put your hands behind your back Miss Bozek," he said, "I'll show it to you for one moment. Don't touch it."

Maria put her hands behind her back. Mr. Bozek took a step forward, ready to launch at the man if he tried to hurt her. The man pulled out a letter. He held it in front of Maria for a moment. She saw her name. It was Helena's handwriting.

CHAPTER 31

The tall man said he'd come back the following evening at the same time. Maria tried everything she could to get the money needed, desperately. But she managed to get only half of it.

Eddie took her aside to the backyard away from their parents. "What are you going to do when that man comes?" he asked.

"I'm going to show him what I have, and plead…"

Eddie shook his head, "He won't accept it, he doesn't sound like…" he sighed. Suddenly Maria saw his eyes becoming moist.

"Eddie, is everything okay?"

He shrugged his shoulders, "Here's two thousand."

Maria looked at the money, shocked. "But Eddie, where from?"

"The deliveries. It's my one year of savings."

"Eddie I can't…—"

"You must. She's my sister too."

Maria bit her lip. "I'll pay you back."

"Don't be a fool. I've been…" he hesitated, "I've been praying for Helena to return. I hope this is a sign."

Maria nodded, her chin quivering. "Eddinka, come here…"

They hugged. Maria shook her head. What a man her little brother had become! They hugged for a long time.

When the tall man knocked on the door again, everyone jumped out of their seats. Helena's father opened the door, and tried a different approach. He pleaded, "We are a poor family, sir." He thanked, "We are so grateful to you for bringing us news." And he even tried flattery, "You must have gone through much, and I can only imagine the dangers you've been through…"

But the man's face was blank. He said nothing. They looked at each other for a long moment. The man said, "You got the money?"

Maria tried to say, "All I got is one thousand, sir…—"

But the man turned around into the night.

"Wait!" Maria exclaimed.

He turned around, halfway.

With trembling hands, Maria handed him the money. He counted it. He gave her the letter and was gone.

Maria took the letter as if it was gold. She knew it was still not an indication that Helena was alive. This could be a letter she wrote in the past, possibly before she was captured.

But during the past twenty-four hours her heart felt lighter. She was hopeful. She *allowed* herself to hope.

She sat in the living room on the sofa, and opened the letter. Her mother came, standing near her, wearing the kitchen apron. Sasha, too, came and sat by her, her feet on the sofa. Eddie stood near the living room's entrance in the hallway. Mr. Bozek came as well.

Maria opened the letter.

Mrs. Bozek exclaimed, "Now don't think you're just going to read it to yourself!"

"Mama," Maria exclaimed, "it's a letter to me!"

Mrs. Bozek shook her head, "It's a letter to all of us. You're a Bozek. We're all Bozeks. Read it out loud, behave!"

Maria cracked a smile. She looked at the letter, "But Mama it's three pages!"

Mrs. Bozek said nothing, her eyebrows raised, and her eyes glaring at Maria.

Maria shook her head and read out loud, "Dear Maria… first things first. That messenger carrying the letter has been very kind to carry it all the way to you.

But please do not…"

Maria's speech slowed down, "…do *not* pay him… anything… because… I've paid him the best… of what I had…"

They heard the door opening. Mr. Bozek called, "Eddie!"

Eddie had ran outside, screaming, "That bastard!"

Mr. Bozek ran after him.

Maria buried her head in her hands, "Oh no… We shouldn't have paid him!"

Sasha exclaimed, "He cheated us!"

But Mrs. Bozek was not impressed by the drama. "Money is money, girls, it comes and goes. Let the men run around trying to prove they're men. We'll keep reading. Go ahead!"

Maria said "Mama!"

"Keep reading I pray!"

Maria nodded.

> "The man promised me full secrecy, and that in case of danger the letter would be destroyed. So I feel free to write to you for the first time in two years in my own name. I'm scared to even pronounce it. I've been Maria for so long now…
>
> For the past eight months I've written you countless of letters, but have not heard from you."

Maria gasped.

> "They say the mail is faulty, but I hope at least one of the letters reached you and that you haven't worried for me throughout this whole time."

Maria began crying. Sasha put her hand on her shoulder. Mrs. Bozek bit her lip. Her eyes were moist.

Maria cleared her throat,

> "I got into trouble at the train station. It's a long story. But I was caught singing a foolish song against the occupying army. We all sang in that office, but I stood near the silly microphone. When I realized it was on, I ran away, just grabbing my purse. Soldiers ran after me into the street. They must have been infuriated... But I somehow made it to the tram. It was the second time the tram had saved me, you would remember well the first time."

Sasha interrupted, "What does she refer to, Maria?"

Maria took a big breath, "Oh, it's not important."

Maria had never told them *how* she got Helena out. She thought they wouldn't have approved.

They heard steps outside, Mr. Bozek came into the house, panting, and sat down in the living room with them, "Nowhere..." he panted, "to be found..."

Eddie came in, "That bastard! He disappeared! We looked all around...!"

Maria pouted her lip, "Eddie, I promise I'll pay you back..."

Eddie shrugged his shoulders, "Well, at least I got to see this old man run," he said and tapped on his father's shoulder, "he sure can run!"

Mrs. Bozek smiled and looked at her husband, "Not only running…"

Sasha exclaimed, "Can we keep reading or what?!"

Maria re-read the section that her father and Eddie missed and then continued,

> "…Soldiers ran after me into the street. They must have been infuriated. But I somehow made it to the tram…"

Maria skipped a line and then continued,

> "I knew I had to flee. I ran into my apartment, grabbed everything into my valise, and left the capital."

Everyone sat at the edge of their seats.

> "I took the train to another town. But I knew the occupying army would mark the name Maria Bozek as problematic… I cannot tell you how sorry I was for my stupidity. I should have never sung that song. I knew things much less serious than that had caused people to disappear. In the new town I fled to, I wrote to you, warning you… I sure hope my mistake had not caused your family any grief, and that you weren't visited by the occupying army…"

Mrs. Bozek exclaimed, "The grace of God!"

Maria nodded. They all did.

She continued,

> "I knew I had to change my identity, and was able to arrange with the money I saved from the train station, a fake marriage. Now my name is Maria Szymczak, and the name Bozek has been erased in my new ID. I was able to procure a new fake high school diploma and other documents."

Mrs. Bozek shook her head, "Resourceful girl."

Maria continued,

> "But I couldn't find work in that town, nor was I safe going back to the capital, nor was coming back to our city an option… So I did something which you might find foolish, but I believe it had saved me."

Sasha said, "What? What?"

Maria read, everyone listening intently,

> "With my new identity I went to the occupying army's placement office for the unemployed. I exhausted all of my money procuring a new name and documents, and knew no one in that town to help me, and was afraid of starving.
>
> So I had to put my ideals aside, and went there. They found allocation for me in a huge laundry factory. But then they told me it was in the occupying country's headquarters."

Eddie jumped, "Impossible!"

Mrs. Bozek yelled at him, "Can we just keep reading without stopping!"

Maria kept reading, breathing heavily,

> "So I was given a train pass, and for two days I travelled to the hated country. I was put in a small apartment with twelve other women laborers, mostly local. Here I've been for the past six months. I cannot tell you of the fear I carry in my heart constantly. I fear I would somehow reveal my real identity while talking in my sleep, or somehow saying something wrong…"

Maria sighed and kept reading,

> "But I do not complain. I have work and basic food, which is more than many have. I think of you everyday, wondering how your family is faring. I pray that your mother had found a good job, and that your father is still employed by the train station."

Mrs. Bozek bit her lip, "The good girl!"

Eddie scolded her, "Mama, don't interrupt!"

Mrs. Bozek stared at him until he looked down. Maria smiled and continued,

> "I constantly think of Eddie and Sashinka (I will call her Sashinka forever, Sasha is too formal for me!) and I hope their school is good, and that they are well.

> Of course, my dearest Maria, I think of you every day. I often feel you, while I work in the factory. I imagine you encouraging me and…"

Maria began choking, but kept reading,

"…encouraging me and pushing me to keep working, even though the work is dull and physically taxing, with the huge pools of hot water and unbelievable piles of uniforms, the size of houses. And the women here are not particularly warm, to say the least. I'm here in my body. But in my mind I'm often on the beach with you, or gossiping about Alexander's new haircut, or with your family in the midnight mass…"

Maria began crying.

They all sat there silently.

Maria sniffled and continued,

"I sure hope, dearest Maria, that I have not done anything to offend you, and that the lack of correspondence is simply due to the mail discrepancies. They do say that mail to the occupied countries is very faulty, and that the intelligence and censorship barely let things through. But I've written to you so many times, and I hate to think none of the letters reached you."

Maria wiped her eyes and read,

"Recently they've been murmuring here about the end of the war coming, and the 'enemy' (the allies) attacking and penetrating the lines. I sure hope that it will happen soon, because every day without seeing you makes my heart ache.

I hate to ask, as I've heard of terrible stories back in the capital, but have you heard anything about my father, mother, or brothers? Reuben was indeed taken with my mother in that second transport, but Solomon and Hannah were still in the enclosure when you smuggled me out... I dread thinking of them. I try, each day, not to think of them, as it brings me unbearable sorrow. But I did want to ask... I know that you would have been the first contact for any of them, had they tried to reach me."

Maria began crying again.

Everyone looked down. Mr. Bozek wiped his tears and cleared his throat.

Maria sobbed and sobbed. Stress that had built in her for months was beginning to dissipate. Sasha rubbed her back.

They all had tears in their eyes.

Maria breathed in heavily, wiped her tears, and kept reading,

"The messenger just told me he needs to leave. I must seal this letter and give it to him. My current address is written below. I'm uncertain if mail can come through, especially from the occupied territories into the main country. But I do have hope: a friend told me that if you address me not in our living quarters, but instead send the letter to the actual *laundry factory*, then chances are high that it shall arrive. So, please, as soon as you receive this letter, let me know your family is safe! Address me as Maria Szymczak, at the factory's address below. I truly hope to hear from you! I cannot explain in words what worry and pain I have, not knowing you and your family are all safe and sound.

Yours, always,

Maria."

Sasha gasped, "She signed with your name?"

Eddie laid back, "She must have still been afraid!"

Mr. Bozek shook his head, "Poor Helena…"

Mrs. Bozek stood up, "I'll prepare some food for her."

Everyone laughed. "Mama!" Sasha said, "She's far away!"

"So what?!" Mrs. Bozek exclaimed, now heading to the kitchen, "We can send food in jars…" She shouted, "We do have some jam! And I can make fish in salt… And pickles! And some salty meat, it can last few weeks if it's in oil… She said she doesn't have food there!"

Maria laughed, "Mama, she didn't say that!"

"I listened to every word," Mrs. Bozek shouted from the kitchen, "She said, '*basic food*', you know what that means? They feed her…" her voice broke, "nothing but potatoes…" she began crying, "She must be starving…"

Mr. Bozek got up to be with her.

Eddie looked at Maria, hesitating. "Can I… write to her too? Can you include a letter from me?"

Sasha jumped, "And from me too!"

Maria smiled, "Of course."

Sasha hugged her. Eddie hesitated, but then joined them too, putting his hand on his big sister.

CHAPTER 32

A week before Maria's 25th birthday, the propaganda-filled radio station of the occupying army suddenly went off the air.

The occupying army in the city tried to keep a "business as usual" appearance. But everyone could sense that something was happening.

Then refugees poured in from the capital. They told of the occupying army retreating, and the liberating allies closing in. The occupying army, while retreating, burned down the capital, and blew up its bridges and many of the historic buildings. The capital was in ruins, refugees said, razed to the ground.

One evening Eddie was infuriated, cursing the occupying army during the family's dinner. The liberating allies were now advancing rapidly toward their city. Liberation felt closer than ever. But Eddie exclaimed, "People say the occupying army would do to us what they've done in the capital!"

Mr. Bozek said nothing. The atmosphere in the

home was tense.

The following day Eddie disappeared. He did not come home that night, nor the following day. Mrs. Bozek was distraught, crying incessantly. Maria tried to calm her down, but to no avail. All Mrs. Bozek was saying was "Eddinka, my Eddinka..."

That night they heard heavy artillery. Guns, machine guns, tanks.

Mr. Bozek brought one of the beds from the living room into their bedroom, and he and Mrs. Bozek slept alongside Maria and Sasha, all crammed in the small room.

But they didn't really sleep. The shooting and the bombardments were unbearable.

At four o'clock in the morning a huge blast rocked the walls of the house. Sasha began crying, "Are we going to die, Papa?"

Mr. Bozek said, "It's all good signs. The liberating allies are here."

They prayed together.

That day Mr. Bozek did not go to work. No one left the house. Mr. Bozek peeked from behind the curtain. The street was empty. Not a soul was out.

They stayed home the whole day. The following day they heard some artillery again, but not as heavy. They had now nearly exhausted all the food in the house.

Mrs. Bozek wanted to go to the market, but Mr. Bozek said, "We'll manage without food. No one is going anywhere."

The day after, they heard noises of cheering in the distance. The ground shook from what sounded like marching. Mr. Bozek said, "I'll go out. Lock the door and let no one in."

The three women looked through the window. But no one was out on the snowy street.

Two hours later Mr. Bozek returned, "The liberating allies are here!"

They cried. Mrs. Bozek fell on her knees, "Thank you God! Now bring our Eddinka home!"

As if answering Mrs. Bozek's prayer, that evening Eddie came home. Never before was he kissed as much. Mrs. Bozek kissed him and hit him alternatingly. "You fool!" she hit him, "I'm so glad you're here!" she kissed him, "I should have locked you inside," she hit him "Thank God you're not hurt!" she kissed him.

Mr. Bozek must have known something. He looked prouder than ever and said, "Tell me everything, don't spare a detail."

Eddie said how he knew that one of his friends, Aleksey, was involved in the resistance movement. "But I wanted to have none of it," he said. "Until what happened in the capital. Then I was… outraged… Seeing the refugees. Papa, Mama, it was… impossible for me not to do anything, and imagine the same happening to us!"

They all listened to him attentively.

"So I came to Aleksey and said that I wanted to enlist. I wasn't the only one. There were many of us. We were trained quickly in a forest. Two days ago we were sent as the back force, covering up a front force going to the northern castle."

Mr. Bozek said, "That's where the army had all their ammunitions…!"

Eddie nodded, "So at night, we infiltrated there, and around four we lit the whole place up from several directions. We blew up their whole bunker. They planned to tear our whole city down as they were retreating. But we took them by surprise."

Mrs. Bozek shrieked, "My hero!"

"Mama," Eddie frowned, "I was at the back lines. I did nothing."

Mrs. Bozek would have none of it, "You helped the front lines. Now our city is saved!"

Eddie sighed. "It was… many were killed. On both sides. But their main reservoir of explosives was gone. Then we joined the liberating allies last night and we marched with them in the morning. The city is finally ours again."

Maria was ecstatic. They went to celebrate in the streets. It seemed as if everyone was out. After these horrific six years of occupation and unheard-of sorrows, no one had to stay inside anymore

But her joy was not complete. She had not heard

back from Helena since she sent her the package, the food jars, the expensive green dress her mother got for her with her best money, and the letters from her and her siblings.

There was now no mail at all between their liberated city and the main occupying country. They were now on different sides of the conflict. She dreaded Helena's state. Would the army there do the same? Burn down factories, evidences of the war efforts?

She felt it too early to celebrate.

CHAPTER 33

University resumed. Maria saw Roman, looking happier than ever, walking with his girlfriend Rebecca.

Maria was happy for them.

But she wasn't at ease.

The weeks passed.

Then, one day when she came home, her mother had a big grin on her face. "You have guests," she said.

"Guests?" Maria exclaimed, "Helena?"

Mrs. Bozek shook her head, "Not Helena," and pointed at the entrance to the living room.

Maria hurried to the living room.

She gasped.

CHAPTER 34

The laundry factory worker, Maria Szymczak, felt the tension growing in the air. Everyone did.

One day the factory manager disappeared.

The following day three of the supervisors also disappeared.

There was unrest in the factory, as new people came to run it.

Spring came. Still there was no mail. She thought of her beloved city, so far away. She heard the allies had conquered it.

To herself she whispered, "It's been liberated!"

But the news did not speak of the territories lost, only of the army realigning and repositioning.

Then there was a rumor about the great leader being killed.

The following day the rumor, passing like fire in the working line, was that the great leader committed suicide. But it was all speculation.

Two days later it was published that the army headquarters had been taken over by the allies.

But it took six more long days until the final news came. Everyone stopped working and listened as the factory's main radio blasted the news:

> "Today, in the early morning, our nation, through the High Command of the Army, officially surrendered to the Supreme Commander of the Allied Expeditionary Force…"

Cries of sorrow passed through the lines. Some of the women wailed. The radio continue blaring:

> "…the Army issued orders to all military, naval and air authorities and to all forces under the control of the High Command to cease active operations as of this morning. The army is obliged to hand over weapons and equipment to the local allied commanders or officers designated by Representatives of the Allied Supreme Commands…"

As the women cried for their country's loss, Helena didn't show any sorrow. She got up, walked out of the factory, went to the nearby woods, fell onto the ground and sobbed.

It was over.

CHAPTER 35

Maria walked into the house. Mrs. Bozek exclaimed, "Maria! Good news!"

Eddie and Sasha looked at Maria excitedly, as Mrs. Bozek handed her the short telegram.

Maria didn't even take off her coat. She turned around and ran out.

Mrs. Bozek yelled, "Where are you going?!"

"I have to let them know Mama! They'll be so happy!!!"

The following morning Maria stood on the platform. She was waiting nervously.

It seemed like forever.

She kept sitting down on the bench, then standing, then walking. Then sitting again. Then standing.

She promised herself she wouldn't cry. Today was,

finally, a happy day.

It was all behind them now.

Helena's heart leapt as her city came into view.

She looked out the windows, absorbing the sights. The buildings. She was so afraid she might see ruins. But she saw none. The buildings were beautiful, shining in the spring sun.

The train slowed down. People inside the train stood up. The platform emerged before her, with countless people standing on it waiting. She took her valise in her hand and straightened her dress—Maria's beautiful green dress.

The train stopped. The doors opened. She waited for a moment and then walked off.

She breathed in the familiar scents. She looked around, hoping to see Maria. Did she receive her telegram? She looked at the many faces, at people greeting other people. Where was…

"Helena!" she heard her name pronounced for the first time in two years. She turned around, and before she knew it she and Maria were embracing, crying, spinning around in pure joy. The rest of the world disappeared.

They sat on the platform. They looked at each other, excited and shy, just as they were on the school's rooftop, so many years earlier, exchanging gifts after the summer break. Then they'd been separated for two months. Now it was two years, though it felt like a lifetime.

Helena had tears in her eyes. They spoke, half sentences, then hugged, then spoke again, then hugged again. They cried on each other's shoulders.

"When you're ready," Maria finally said, "I have a surprise for you!"

"What is it?" Helena asked nervously.

"Solomon, he made it…—"

"Solomon?!" Helena screamed, "He is alive?!"

Maria nodded, tears in her eyes, "They came to me a few weeks ago."

"They?"

"He and Hannah."

"Oh Maria!"

Maria laughed and cried, "He reacted just like you when I…" she sniffled, "when I told… when I told him you were safe…"

Helena shook her head, "I knew it. I knew he'd survive!"

Maria nodded, "He was able to get your old house back, the big one, Helena, from before the war! He told me to bring you there when you come, he didn't want to leave Hannah…"

"Is she…" Helena's eyes widened, "is she injured? Sick?"

Maria shook her head, her eyes filled with tears, "No, she's pregnant, Helena. She's due to give birth any day now…"

Helena stood up, "Maria, what good news…!"

Maria nodded and stood up, "I'll go there with you. They are waiting for us."

Helena nodded, tears streaming down her cheeks. She grabbed Maria's hands, "Don't you ever leave me again you hear me!"

Maria nodded, "I promise. Do you promise?"

Helena nodded, "I promise."

EPILOGUE

Helena Goldstein and Maria Bozek were never separated again. They remained close friend through the decades. Helena Goldstein became a successful accountant. Among her clients was a pharmacy owned by Maria Bozek-Nowak.

Four decades after the war ended, Helena Goldstein passed away at the age of 66. Near her bedside stood her longtime friend, Maria Bozek-Nowak.

Maria Bozek-Nowak dedicated her later years to educating children and teens about friendship and world peace. According to her, "The most important thing to understand is that there is no difference between people. Under our skin we're all the same. If you understand this, you will do whatever it takes to help other people when they are in need."

In 1995, Maria Bozek-Nowak was recognized by the state of Israel as Righteous Among the Nations. As of 2017, Maria Bozek-Nowak still lectures and speaks of love between the nations, now at the age of 97.

This book is dedicated to the memory of the Goldstein family members and to all of those who perished during the Holocaust.

Likewise, it is dedicated to the Bozek family, and to all of the 20,000 Righteous Among the Nations, who saved the lives of innocent people throughout the Holocaust, serving as miracle-workers in times of great darkness. Their light will shine forever.

THE END.

PHOTOGRAPHS

Maria Bozek with her brother Edmund, Krakow, c. 1928

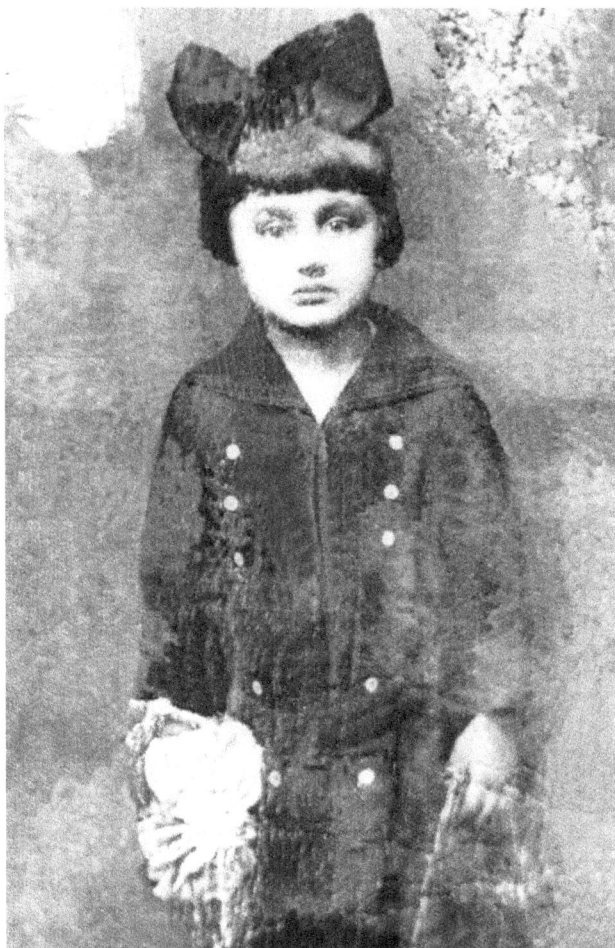

The only preserved photograph of Helena Goldstein as
a young girl, Krakow, c. 1925

Helena Goldstein, picture for her High school diploma,
Krakow, 1938

Maria Bozek, picture for her High school
diploma, Krakow, 1938

CLAIM YOUR GIFT!

Thank you for purchasing this novel. For a special behind-the-scenes e-book, including historical background on which *The Sisterhood* was based please visit:

Books.click/Sisterhood

* * *

This e-book companion includes group discussion ideas, unique photographs and much more!

JOIN OUR ONLINE BOOK CLUB!

Book club members receive free books and the hottest pre-release novels. To join our exclusive online book club and discuss *The Sisterhood* with likeminded readers, please visit:

Books.click/DuboisBookclub

* * *

We look forward to see you in our bookclub family!

RATE THIS BOOK!

We thank you for taking a quick moment to rate this book online. Let others know what you thought at this easy link!

Books.click/SisterhoodRating

The author has requested that we include the following personal email address below. Readers are invited to contact author Caroline Dubois directly at the following address. The author attempts to answer each and every email from dedicated readers.

AuthorCarolineDubois1@gmail.com

NOVELS BY CAROLINE DUBOIS:

All the Uncried Tears

The Stolen Violin

The Sisterhood

Her Father's Daughter

The Friendship

Islam

The Secret Earpiece

www.ingramcontent.com/pod-product-compliance
Lightning Source LLC
Chambersburg PA
CBHW071933090426
42740CB00011B/1690